HERTFORDSHIRE LIBRARY SERVICE

Please return this book on or before the last
date shown or ask for it to be renewed

L32/rev79

OUR ADMIRAL

OUR ADMIRAL

A Biography of
Admiral of the Fleet
EARL BEATTY

by
Charles Beatty

W. H. ALLEN · LONDON
A Howard & Wyndham Company
1980

Printed and bound in Great Britain by
W & J Mackay Limited, Chatham, Kent
for the Publishers W. H. Allen & Co. Ltd,
44 Hill Street, London W1X 8LB

ISBN 0 491 02388 X

Of dauntless physical and moral courage; in moments of crisis his brain worked with absolute clarity; his judgement was sound and his decisions were the result of careful reflection.

D.N.B. (Concise)
Pt.2. article
BEATTY, David.

If one takes at random any figure in history and softens or hides his background, the result is to change the whole character and meaning of what he said and did.

Foster (F): *The Perennial Religion*
(Regency Press 1969)

CONTENTS

ACKNOWLEDGEMENTS

Over the years a very large number of people have been kind enough to talk to me about our Admiral, many of whom have passed on and others slipped through the meshes of memory. In connection with the preparation of the present work I have been fortunate in obtaining advice, assistance, access to material, criticism and suggestions from many sources. I am particularly grateful to the following:—

Lady Ainsworth, Miss I. M. Austen, M.B.E., W.R.N.S., Diana Lady Avebury, David the third Earl Beatty, Joan Temple Beatty my wife, Beken of Cowes Ltd., Captain Alan Black, R.N., Martin Campbell, City of Cork Archives, City of Portsmouth Archives, Captain John Ehrman, R.N., Sir Gerald Glover, Hampshire Library Service, London Library, Christopher Mead, the following Museums, National Army, Imperial War, Maritime (Greenwich), Naval Historical Library, Naval Records Society, Mr and Mrs Nutting, Commander Ouvry, D.S.O., R.N., Office of Works St Paul's Cathedral, Alfred Philp, R.N., and the following Public Records Offices at Chancery, Kew, St Catherine's, Michael Purton, Dr Rex Roberts, Captain Stephen Roskill, R.N., Lt. Cmdr. Charles Stuart, R.N., John Towndrow, Lieut. E. G. Wye, R.N. For accurate presentation of the final typescript I am obliged to Trans Promotions Ltd., of Hythe, Hampshire. The B.B.C. Hulton Picture Library for their permission to use the photographs in this book.

AUTHOR'S NOTE

In 1933 our Admiral, David Richard Beatty who was my father's younger brother, agreed that because of my knowledge of the family, I might one day write his biography, 'If Winston doesn't'. Circumstances prevented me from making a start and he died three years later, but I continued to take an interest in everything concerning him.

Then as now my aim is not so much to establish his place in history as to project the frank and faithful image of an extraordinary character from a point of view which is surely unusual and may be unique. Such an image or portrait requires clear definition lest the bold outline become blurred by detail. Peripheral elements are therefore excluded unless they bear on his character, and this particularly applies to battlefields, whether at sea, on land, or across the council table. All such aspects have been dealt with by distinguished authors, most of whose works I have been able to consult, and for which I am truly grateful.

Apart from the oustanding biography by Rear-Admiral Chalmers (1951) only one Life was published, by Geoffrey Rawson (about 1933), and that was not commissioned. Nor was the Chalmers *opus* 'definitive', as he himself notes in his Preface:—

> 'It is too near his (the Admiral's) lifetime to reveal all that he wrote
> . . . The day may come, however, when the historian will be glad
> to make full use of them (the letters); for it is certain that future
> generations will want to know more about the man who was not
> only Britain's greatest fighting Admiral in the World War of
> 1914–1918, but also the most effective First Sea Lord who ever stood
> up before the Cabinet as the champion of British sea-power.'

Chalmers was originally intended, by the second Earl, to do the Service record while Sir Shane Leslie dealt with the personal Life; but the latter found the conditions under which he worked were incompatible with his integrity as a writer. On talking the matter over with me he decided to withdraw and Admiral Chalmers took over completely.

With the aim of publishing a Definitive Life the second Earl next commissioned Captain Roskill, R.N., and he was promised a free hand; only to be abruptly dropped on the absurd ground that he had been personally responsible for the publication of the Harper Report on the Battle of Jutland which the Admiral was alleged to have suppressed for disreputable reasons. Roskill was then Vice-Chairman of the Naval Records Society, but the decision to publish the Report was a collective, not a personal one. Even so, Roskill had no alternative but to withdraw.

At this period I had a domestic upheaval which meant there was no longer a secure place for the letters and other things which had come down to me from my ancestors, particularly my grandfather, the Admiral's father. Many of the letters I offered to the second Earl, but he was not interested, so, knowing that a collector would look after them, they were sold. Soon afterwards my Agent suggested I should make a start on the Life as he had a Publisher interested. So I tried to trace the letters and found they had been bought at auction. Here is the buyer's reply:

Frank Partridge & Sons Ltd
144–146 New Bond Street
London W.1

13th February 1964

Dear Mr Beatty,

I thank you for your letter of the 11th February with regard to Admiral Beatty's letters which I bought at Sotheby's on the 27th May 1963. These have now passed into the possession of the present Lord Beatty. His address is Chichley (sic) Hall, Newport Pagnell, Bucks., and I would suggest you write direct to him. I know he is very amenable to showing any letters with regard to his family.

Yours sincerely,
John Partridge.

Confidently I wrote as instructed and said I was ready to start, being relieved that he had those letters after all. He never replied, so, like Sir Shane Leslie, Stephen Roskill, and, later, John Barnes, I had no alternative but to withdraw. Of these distinguished writers, Leslie was an old friend, and when he found his brief incompatible with his integrity he talked the matter over with me before leaving the scene. In due course he bequeathed all his relevant papers to Captain Roskill at Churchill College, Cambridge, where they have a magnificent naval archives collection.

Next to be commissioned was John Barnes, Lecturer in Political Science at the London School of Economics and a Member of the Naval Records Society. He too became uneasy about the conditions imposed, and when we discussed the issue I formed the impression that he would pull out. When his book failed to appear I felt free to ask the third Earl, who succeeded in June 1972, for an unequivocal warrant to restart my project. In a letter dated 31st July 1978 he gave it:—

'Everything you want will be at your disposal, and arrangements can be made, either to copy papers or to take them away, if absolutely required, for which you have my permission, although the Trustees and Executors did stress that they would prefer that the papers were not removed.'

Despite this open door it was not surprising to find that the policy of censorship begun by the Admiral, and perpetuated to the third generation by his executors, persisted. Fortunately, I already had much of the material required for a 'family portrait', and the rest was not difficult to acquire.

Charles Beatty
Ghuznee House
Hampshire

I
ANCESTRAL VOICES

Some people inherit a genetic package of explosive potential, often through intermarriage over many generations within a close-knit group. Of these a few reach great heights, but many come to grief. One who succeeded was the second child of an obscure Irish country gentleman who ran off with the wife of a senior officer in his own regiment, and lived to regret it.

The boy, David Beatty, grew up to command the greatest battle fleet in history, become a hero and a legend, wealthy and well-beloved. Yet his whole life was under a family bane which dogged him until high office became a burden and private life a cage. His secret has never been told, and even now is revealed only because there is no one still extant who can be hurt; and, without it, to understand the depth of the Admiral's character is virtually impossible. It is equally difficult to appreciate his motives, particularly in relation to the Service when he seemed to be acting obstinately against his own best interests, without knowing the manner of his birth, six months before his parents were married.

'The "Law of Arms" as it affects the achievement[1] of a bastard is in line with Common Law, according to which the unfortunate child comes into the world without parents, without a blood relation of any degree, and without a name. With this general handicap, he obviously comes into the world without any right of inheritance.' (Franklyn (J): *Shield and Crest*, 1967.)

Now that such children can be retrospectively legitimised, the severity of disapproval in the last century may seem absurd, but such a view fails to take account of the practical motive behind it:

[1] The bar sinister. See Appendix 'B'.

preservation of landed property by inheritance. Among royalty there have always been exceptions, for the 'divine right' was above the law. To a lesser extent nobility also tolerated 'natural' children, but to County families, and particularly the squirearchy of Protestants in Ireland, bastardy was a serious offence; not only against morality. For if such interlopers were permitted any legal standing they might subvert the social order created and maintained by their interrelated families, and so imperil the continuity of estates which has passed from father to son for centuries. Since such properties also passed 'across' through marriage to an heiress, illegitimacy was of equal concern for daughters whose prospects might be in jeopardy should any doubt arise as to their entitlement.

For which reason David's parents had to make sure of the silence of those few who knew about his premature arrival, and thereafter made it as difficult as possible for anyone else to discover the truth. In this they were surprisingly successful. It is a tribute to both of them that, from their secret marriage until the two boys grew up and had to be told, no one outside the tail male[1] ever did find out; with the exception of their father's widow by his second marriage.

David Richard Beatty was born on 17th January 1871 at Howbeck Lodge, Stapeley, in the Registration District of Nantwich, County of Chester. His father, David Longfield Beatty, Gentleman, in person registered the birth, giving the mother's name as Edith Catherine Beatty, formerly Sadlier. Registration took place on 17th February.

The Certificate is surprising for two reasons in particular. No one in the family, still less outside it, as for instance in Naval circles, seems to have discovered that the future Admiral was Richard as well as David. His father, for obvious reasons, gave his mother's name as Beatty, when in fact she was still Mrs Chaine. He was entitled to do this because there was no fraudulent intent. Indeed, it amounts to an undertaking to marry Edith as soon as she was free.

REGISTRATION DISTRICT OF LIVERPOOL

Application Number 7513 H 1871 marriage solemnised at St

[1] Charles Harold Longfield Beatty.

2

Michael's Church in the Parish of Liverpool in the County of Lancaster.

No. 28 Married June 2nd David Beatty age 30, Bachelor of 56 Mount Pleasant, father's name David Vandeleur Beatty, Gentleman. Catherine Edith Sadlier age 27 Spinster of Howbeck, Nantwich, father's name Nicholas Sadlier, Gentleman.

Married according to the rites and ceremonies of the Established Church by licence by me Fredk Brealey in the presence of James Barrow, Jane Barrow.

Certified to be a true copy of a Register of Marriages in the district above mentioned. Given at the General Register Office, London, under the Seal of the said Office, the 17th day of August, 1978.

There would have been no wedding breakfast. Bride and Groom must have hurried home, – to Howbeck Lodge, for 56 Mount Pleasant would be a fictitious address designed to conceal the fact that they were already living together – there to be greeted by Charlie, a year old, and David, nearly six months. The entire proceeding is highly irregular.

For instance, there could have been no question of putting up the banns, for there must have been individuals eager to respond to the parson's admonition, 'If any of you know cause, or just impediment, why these two persons should not be joined together in holy matrimony, ye are to declare it.' Marriage by licence dispensed with banns, but forced Edith to make a false declaration as to her status because a divorced woman could not be married in church. Then there was the matter of witnesses. Either they knew the truth and dissembled, or did not and compounded the deception. Clearly it would have been imprudent to invite anyone to be a witness who was not a total stranger, in which case it would not occur to him, or her, that there was anything out of order. It may safely be concluded therefore that the Barrows signed the certificate in good faith, probably never having seen the principals before.

As for the bridegroom, the price he had to pay was a burden on his conscience which grew heavier with years and passed to his heirs, who, when two more boys came along, could have been disinherited by the younger, legitimate, children.

The bride's resolute character carried her through all this and would succeed in dominating both her husband and her children; in the only surviving portrait, a water-colour, she appears at first sight almost frail, but closer study reveals traits of determination which would have done credit to the Admiral. She wears a black riding habit with a white collar under the high neck. The face is flawless, oval, and pale under a pile of very fair hair, plaited and coiled to fit under a top hat when out hunting. There is only a trace of eyebrows, and the blue eyes, for all their femininity have a glance which could hold anyone's. The mouth though soft is rather wide, the lower lip decisive, as if about to speak in the manner of one who expects to be obeyed. Her eldest boy, Charles must have been so like her, particularly in hair colour, – in contrast to David's black – that had he been a girl they could have passed for sisters. Indeed, the contrast between parents and these two children implies an unusual genetic package. The boys so alike in temperament, but contrasting in looks, and both short: about five foot five, with small hands and feet. Their father was six foot four and of a quite different cast of countenance, with very long arms and legs, big hands and feet.

To appreciate the magnitude of the scandal which led to the marriage it is necessary to bear in mind the intolerance of County families. They were almost invariably Army as well, the eldest sons vowed to Mars from birth, so their petty dynasties were equally concerned with property and rank, a dual qualification represented by the phrase 'an officer and a gentleman' which sums up their code of honour. If it was unbecoming for a gentleman to partake of another's wife, it was almost a breach of Field Service Regulations for an officer to steal his Colonel's Lady. Yet this is what happened, and, even now, the essential circumstances can be reconstructed.

Like other regiments, particularly cavalry, the 4th Hussars were often in Ireland because of continuing unrest which culminated in the Fenian uprisings. The worst of these, almost a civil war, occurred in 1867 and involved not only Dublin, Drogheda and Kerry but also Liverpool and Manchester. Unfortunately for them the rebels had no cavalry.

William Chaine had bought his Commission as Ensign on the

19th December 1856, six years before David Longfield Beatty bought his; so Chaine was considerably senior: a serious matter when promotion required so many years service in successive ranks. By December 1868, when the romance between David and Edith was already on the boil, Chaine bought himself the rank of Major while Beatty had progressed only to Lieutenant (also bought). He became Captain, and that honorary, on retirement, 21st November 1865, having seen no active service.

At this period his father David Vandeleur Beatty, 'The Old Master', 1815–1881, still resided at the eighteenth century mansion Borodale, County Wexford, to which he had moved from his own place, Healthfield on the river Slaney, a few miles away to the south, sold for reasons of economy; for why run two houses when one will do? The Captain had been born at Borodale and spent his early life there, so he was within reach of parental wrath when it became evident that Edith would not give him up. So obstinate did she appear that The Old Master, no doubt backed up by Chaine, pushed his erring son off to India 'to forget'; but he did not stay long. Chaine remained in the Army List until 1st October 1877, six years after Edith re-married, when he too sold his Commission to become an honorary Lieutenant-Colonel, two grades up on Beatty.

Letters from India preserved at Borodale showed her persistent importunity: 'Be *satisfied*, Edith, – I love *you*'. She was not satisfied and he had to go back to her, caught on the one hand between love and duty, on the other between his parents and her husband: a classic example of conflicting loyalties. The rigid code demanded that he obey his father, respect Edith's status, and avoid or at least conceal, open rivalry which a few decades earlier would have led to a duel. Against all that was his personal, irrevocable commitment to Edith, and to this she lent her own considerable strength of character. Between them they challenged the Establishment and its morality, regardless of the cost to themselves. He took her away from the now hostile environment, in which both had been brought up, and found refuge somewhere in Cheshire where he had friends among horsemen who would back the 'dash of a cavalry-man' against all odds.

Neither could have had much confidence that Chaine would institute divorce proceedings. He must have been hoping that his wife's infatuation would be exorcised by the changed and disagreeable circumstances in which she now found herself. His only problem was that, if she became contrite, would he be under an obligation to take her back? And if so, would he want her?

Such maverick behaviour on the part of Captain Beatty suggests a streak of eccentricity which became more marked in later life, the origin of which must have been among previous generations, which, from the eighteenth century, were closely related to other families within the pale of the Plantation. This genetic time-bomb had been armed by his father when he married a young, raven-haired beauty who was also a considerable heiress, Mary Longfield of Longueville, County Cork, his first cousin. As the future Admiral's grandmother she endowed him with consanguinous blood which in other scions led not to fame, or fortune.

She died in 1848 when the future Captain was seven, and by the boy's twenty-first birthday, his father had re-married twice, the second time to Margaret Charlotte Alcock of Wilton (1851), the daughter of a near and wealthy neighbour whose extravagant modern castle, complete with moat and battlements, was but half an hour's drive from Borodale. The matter is not without influence on the Captain's character, for he hardly knew his mother, and relations with his stepmothers are not likely to have been genial. Even without a scandal, and a sinister circumstance far removed from the mundane, Mary Longfield bought something more to Borodale than the fortune which temporarily saved it from decline and fall: a mystery which has never been solved.

Whatever the truth, she does seem to have left behind a shadowy influence which sometimes could be baneful; perhaps derived from something much further back, and of which her son could not fail to be aware; though it would hardly have occurred to him that the bane would persist during the lives of some of his descendants, including the future Admiral. It is an eerie feeling to reflect that half one's blood comes from a mother who apparently returned from the dead.

The little church of Killurin, near Healthfield, preserved a burial register for its tiny churchyard, in which the family vault occupies the south-east corner. The register twice states that Mrs David Beatty was there interred. The first entry is for 1846, aged twenty-nine, the second for 1848, aged thirty-two. It has been argued that they must refer to different 'Mrs David Beattys', one

the wife of him of Healthfield, the other of his son at Borodale.
Now, David of Healthfield (1787–1855) was succeeded by his
son, David of Borodale (1815–1881). Thus there were twenty-
eight years between them, and, as the elder died at sixty-eight, the
younger at sixty-six, for many years they were contemporaries:
and so were their wives.

Against that we have the fact that Mary Longfield did come to
live at Borodale, after the death of the much older Mrs David
Beatty of Healthfield, who married in 1813, twenty-five years
before her own wedding. That being the case, the entries could
refer to the same woman, who returned to the vault in 1848. After
the mourners had dispersed and the flowers removed from
underground, there would have been no workmen available to
replace, and seal against seepage, the great stone slab at the head of
the steps. Instead, the iron grille at the bottom of the steps would
have been locked. Had it so remained, then Mary could not have
been roused, or, if she was, could hardly have survived. This is
where legend begins to seem credible, at least in essence; for it
claims that someone not only had access to the key but also knew
that Mary was still wearing a diamond ring which would not
come off when she was laid out. An obvious suspect was the
butler, for the key was kept in his pantry and he would have
known about the ring. Also he would have been free to come and
go as he pleased. The story goes that he went to the vault during
the night following the funeral, opened the coffin, and, failing to
pull off the ring, cut into the knuckle. Blood spurted. Mary
stirred. He ran. He has not been seen since, and there is the legend
of a 'running butler' which used to be widely believed from
Waterford to Cornwall.

The tale continues that she walked home, in her shroud, but
this is hardly credible as the house is at least a mile from the
churchyard by road, though there might in those days have been a
short cut. So, if we allow that blood-letting roused her – which it
might well do by lowering intracranial pressure – she would still
be in a bad way. Therefore, unless more than one ghoul was
involved, we may also suppose that, overcome by remorse and in
panic fear of divine retribution, the wretched man went to
Healthfield for help. No doubt he had a horse tethered nearby,
intended for his escape. It would take only a few minutes to raise
the alarm, a few more for rescuers to arrive; but in that time she

could have sufficiently recovered to appreciate her situation.

One further clue remains. As she had no daughter the ring is said to have passed to the Captain and thence to the only daughter of that generation, Kathleen Roma who was known as 'Trot', who claimed she had it. As she in turn had no daughter, Trot said she would leave it to the Tail Male. That it never reappeared after her death has not caused me any regrets. On a happier note, there does survive a tear-locket which her widower had made: of crystal surrounded by gold. In a most delicate incised script it bears not only a striking tribute to her, but also an aphorism which may be intended to refer to the mystery:—

> *Remember Mary Longfield and the 18th of May 1848*
> *Her dying excellence deserves a tear.*
> *Her fond remembrance still is cherished here.*
> *She was like thee: She life possessed.*
> *And time will be when thou shalt rest.*

Could 'thee' refer to Mary herself? No one will ever know, but in view of the equation of death with rest one may conjecture that she did not achieve it in the vault, if indeed she had been previously interred; but that her devoted widower believed, no doubt passionately, that rest was now her due.

A question then arises. Was her body taken back to Killurin or had it never been there? Certainly, no subsequent member of the family occupied the vault. Instead, they were buried in ordinary graves of the parish of Bree, with which they had no direct connection.

In 1933, as owner of the vault, I tried to arrange for it to be opened, in the hope of finding some clue to the mystery, such as an empty coffin. Understandably perhaps, in view of Irish superstition, no one would come forward to move the great stone slab covering the steps down. I took no further action and no one else is entitled to do so; so the vault keeps its secret: if any.

Mary's eldest was seven when the locket was made, and by the usual convention already destined for the Army; like his predecessors, particularly grandfather, who at his own expense raised a cavalry troop called the Healthfield Horse, for service in the Peninsular war, where in 1809, at the age of twenty-two he was awarded the Telavera medal. His son, the Admiral's grandfather, served in the Crimea and held the Sevastopol medal (1854), so the Captain's career was apparently determined from birth. It was not, however, to develop at all conventionally, nor provide opportunities for martial arts. Though he did start off with the advantage of being a student at Heidelburg University, where his exceptionally long reach made him a successful duellist among those who fought for the honour of being blooded, leaving a permanent facial cicatrice from the traditional sabre (*schlager*). This was not to the Irishman's taste, he bore no scar. Whatever his record, he certainly acquired a business sense which later on would prove most useful, as did preliminary military training.

Since Queen Victoria's marriage to Albert of Saxe-Coburg-Gotha, in 1840, all things Teutonic were in fashion, and it is not surprising, therefore, that on leaving the University, the Captain was allowed to purchase the Queen's Commission, in a crack regiment at the age of twenty-one. Seven years after that, on 14th April 1869, when he and Edith were already living together, in Cheshire, her husband belatedly filed a petition for divorce, and in the same year the Captain sold his Commission. The decree nisi was granted on 22nd July 1870 and the Absolute followed on 21st February '71. So it took three months to arrange for the marriage.

Was his resignation voluntary? In one sense the answer must be affirmative, since it was his own choice. In another sense it cannot have been so; for even if the matter of the divorce was not yet common gossip, it would soon be an outstanding scandal in his 'set'; for there could be no hiding the fact that he was 'living in sin'. And the 'sin' was of a particularly audacious nature because the lady was the wife of a senior officer in his own regiment.

Fortunately, the loss of pay was no longer a critical matter; for his eye to business, combined with a real flair for horsemanship and horses, made him largely independent of his father. Which was just as well, since the Borodale estate was running down owing to The Old Master's extravagant life-style; largely due to insistance that he must have his own pack of hounds. If the scandal did not directly cause a breach with his parents, the Captain seldom returned to Borodale until he inherited, many years later; and one may safely conclude that he would have been no more welcome there than in the bosom of his regiment; wherein he had seen no active service, no doubt to his lasting regret.

The celebrated sporting cartoonist GAF made a watercolour drawing of him at this period or somewhat later. It gives the impression of a belligerent thruster intent upon an unseen quarry and determined to carry it off, regardless of opposition or competition. The loose, lanky figure wears a brown cutaway riding jacket, with tails, over a white waistcoat with a narrow grey check; fawn breeches, brown leggings and black boots. He stands facing the light with a menacing shadow on the ground behind him. The left hand is deep in a breeches pocket. The right holds a thin cane with its tip touching the ground. The dark eyes have a piercing, hawk-like, quality under the truncated topper: a hat he had specially made for him to mitigate the impression of height.

What can be seen of his hair is very dark and, for those days, rather thick, though it does not touch the collar at the back. A black walrus moustache, frowning bushy eyebrows and neatly trimmed sideboards confirm the impression of a predator poised for action. This despite a formal white stock with large gold pin. Is it only coincidence that the horseshoe points down? He must have known that means 'your luck is running out', but he would not believe anything of the sort could happen; not now that, despite formidable opposition, he had pretty well everything he wanted, including respectability. As for the boys' secret, no need to worry about that yet; and the longer it could be kept the less the chances of embarrassment.

Even so, the childhood of Charles and David was overshadowed by something which affected their parents' moods, and, even before they went to boarding school, they must at least have known there was a rift between parents and grandparents, though no one would discuss it, still less explain how it came about. In fact the rift never did heal, and, though outwardly assured, the strain on both Edith and her David soon began to tell. She became over possessive. He became eccentric, irrascible, tyrannous.

Although until the 1930's he was still in living memory, some of which persisted, – chiefly through his widow, to reach the next generation, of the boys' childhood few traces remain. Though many of their letters were preserved by Edith, most were subsequently destroyed before the boys became sufficiently distinguished to make it seem likely that almost anything connected with them might be worth keeping. We can, however, visualise the sort of early training they went through, beginning with the routine of stables, to which they would have been subject when straight out of the nursery. It was usual for any child to ride almost as soon as he could walk, though instead of a saddle he had a bucket seat.

Both fathers and schoolmasters regarded boys as 'wild'; like horses to be 'broken' before they could be 'made'. It follows that the principle of education was not so much inculcation of knowledge as die-stamping character into an acceptable mould, designed by and for the social hierarchy. This in turn was based, about equally, on distinctions of rank and of family. Sporting prowess (hunting, shooting and racing) came third, and money, or the lack of it, was an almost unmentionable subject in polite conversation. Even so, the system did produce officers of personal integrity, physical toughness and professional competence; all of them rooted, of necessity, in moral and physical courage.

For David the process of being moulded began in infancy and became a matter of Service discipline at the tender age of eleven and a half, when he entered Burney's Naval Academy (a 'crammer') at Gosport. Thence he emerged as a cadet: his feet on the lowest rung of the naval ladder which he would climb to the top, at a time when it was much longer than it ever was before, or since. In 1884 he was posted to H.M. Training Ship *Britannia*,[1] moored in the river Dart with another man-of-war, *Hindustan*; below where the modern Naval College (Dartmouth) now stands and compared to the comforts of which these two old warships would have seemed like prison hulks. So began our Admiral's nautical saga, and not badly, for, despite his poor start he managed to be tenth on the passing-in list, out of thirty-two.

Living conditions in *Britannia* would in these days cause a riot, yet were evidently tolerated by the young gentlemen. Were it not so, David's letters home would have some comment, or even complaint, instead of, by their omission, implying that he was tough enough to take it. And he was already extrovert, even aggressive. One report says he resented discipline. Another rates him for skylarking, which being interpreted means he was already up against both adult authority and student bullies. Equally typical in the light of later of later developments is the implication

[1] See Appendix 'E'.

that he knew how far to go without losing his place in the all-important queue: for promotion. He may even have surmised, thanks to his father, that, as with horses, trainers have better hopes for a single wild one (with the right blood and conformation) than for a whole string of docile animals.

The two wooden men-o'-war still wore their horizontal black bands '*á la Nelson*' between the lines of gun ports, but the effect was spoilt by additional decks, surmounted by ugly wooden superstructure. The bows of *Britannia* invested *Hindustan*'s stern. How are the mighty fallen! For the former dated back to 1762. She was a ship of the line with a hundred guns, and had been fourth in the wake of *Victory* at Trafalgar. By that time she was almost as famous a name, if for a strange reason. In 1779 at Spithead she was the scene of a court martial presided over by five admirals and eight captains. The accused, charged with misconduct at the battle of Ushant, was Admiral Keppel, who was immensely popular in the fleet. Not only was he aquitted, the President of the Court declared the charges, 'unfounded and malicious'. On hearing which – or rather getting it by flag signal – every ship at anchor fired a salute.

Amidships, *Britannia* now had to wear a crowning shame, a substantial smoke-stack, more like a factory chimney than anything nautical. Presumably the course was made as short as possible, partly because conditions were so harsh and partly because cadets could be relied on to work harder than they would if living soft.

Beatty was there for two and a half years, and seems to have taken it all in his stride. He was never one to complain and, although small for his age, was a bonny fighter. The earliest letter to survive was written when he was fourteen, on octavo paper with the *Britannia* letterhead in blue and her embossed symbol at the top of the page, with helmet, trident and round shield, as she appeared on the old pennies and indeed any context for Britain's 'Sure Shield', the Royal Navy.

Some years earlier Prince George went through the same mill and bitterly complained to his father, King Edward VII, of the systematic bullying, the hard lying, and the way he was cheated by the bigger boys of what little pocket money he was allowed. 'It never did me any good to be a Prince, and many was the time I wished I hadn't been'. Cadet Beatty, on the other hand was chiefly concerned to acquire ten shillings from his father, ostensibly as a present for his Instructor, and his only grouse was that there had been no fighting during a local election.

Indeed, fighting was the boys' principal activity out of school hours, and bullying as such was only one aspect of it. As for the curriculum, it was by no means all in terms of seamanship. Mathematics came first, principally as applied to navigation, then physics of an elementary sort, followed by religious instruction for the Church by law established. Less attention was paid to French, naval history and signals.

29th November 1885

Dearest Mama,

I hope that you and all at home are well, and that Father is better and able to hunt again. It is a long time since I have heard from you, nearly a month, so I don't know anything about you, so please write soon and tell me. I suppose everybody is busy now working for the Election. They were electing down here yesterday, but I don't know which has got in yet.[1] I don't think there was much of a row. I went on leave to Paignton yesterday to Mrs Patrick: she is very nice and kind and blows you out like anything. It has been very wet down here lately. We have not been able to get out at all today, it having rained all the time. The term was photographed the other day: thirty-two cadets ought to have been, but owing to illness and being expelled, there were only twenty-nine cadets. I being among them. Our class want to give our Instructor a present, so will you please send me ten shillings to subscribe to it, and then I will get some photographs with it as well. Work is going on as usual: last Wednesday was our essay exam. We had three hours writing as hard as we could, after which my fingers were awfully stiff, then as Wednesday was wet I worked the whole afternoon as well. Have you had any good runs lately or does the frost stop you much? Only four weeks more, it will soon be over. With best love to all at home I remain

Your loving son,

David Beatty

[1] Lord Salisbury formed the next Government.

Cadet Beatty completed the course without major trouble and went home to await the dramatic moment of his first posting, on which the rest of his career would depend. It came in January 1886 in a most unexpected form: China Station. To his temperament nothing could have been more welcome than the promise of adventure in foreign waters when most of his term would still be ashore or with the Channel Fleet. His mother, understandably, took a different view; and with reason. Even without her Irish temperament, any mother would have been shocked; though few would have the courage, or the connections, to challenge the Admiralty's order. Ever since the Summer Palace of the Emperor had been sacked, twenty years before, in reprisal for the torture of British Officers, the Chinese were detested as devious, treacherous and exceedingly cruel. That young David might fall into their hands did not bear thinking about.

By this time the Captain had given up Howbeck Lodge and acquired a more extensive establishment for training and racing: The Moat, near Rugby. It was from there that Edith addressed her protest, to no less a personage than Admiral Sir Charles Beresford, Fourth Sea Lord. As such he was in a position to reprimand whoever had been responsible for that callous – as it appeared to Edith – exile of a boy to the ends of the Earth. Nor was that all, for in his capacity as Member of Parliament for Waterford, he would also be able to ask awkward questions in the House; a habit which, carried to excess, later made him unpopular with the Navy.

Not that Beresford would have welcomed Edith's spirited protest. True, he could hardly ignore it since he was a friend of the family and must have stayed at Borodale; but to take resolute action could be embarrassing for himself, should the Admiralty stand firm. In fact her *démarche* was successful beyond all expectation, for the Cadet was sent to the most desirable, exclusive and prestigious post in the Fleet: a circumstance for which he would be grateful all his life. *Alexandra*, flagship of Admiral the Duke of Edinburgh,[1] Commander-in-Chief Mediterranean Station was widely known as 'the favourites ship', not always in mockery, for the Duke was a fine, professional sea-dog, intolerant of inefficiency.

[1] Queen Victoria's second son.

In facilitating this appointment no doubt Beresford checked David's record, particularly from *Britannia*; but he would also have relied on the family's Service tradition and social standing. Nor had he anything to lose, for the Admiralty branch responsible for postings could have chosen otherwise. Thus, if young David failed to make a name for himself Beresford could not be blamed, but if he did, then the eccentric Admiral M.P. would gain much of the credit.

Despite her royal master and gilded company, *Alexandra* was out of date, being a three-master with only auxiliary steam; and no doubt the Royal Duke would have hoisted his flag elsewhere had it not been for the impending Jubilee Review in the following year, 1887, which brought together off Spithead the best, biggest and newest men-o'-war their Lordships could muster for an unprecedented and overwhelming pageant of sea power. Whether some of her crew were favourites in any sense prejudicial to good order and naval discipline is extremely doubtful, though individuals with impressive connections might prosper more than others. And why not in those days? Service rank was one standard, social status another. When both were justified by performance there was the best of all chances of rapid promotion. Even the Chaplain became a bishop.

Though there was then no likelihood of David ever having a title the fact that he soon had the *entrée* to the royal circle ashore made up for the lack, and when, in May, he became Midshipman: an officer now, no longer a boy, he could not have been better placed; no matter what his qualifications or background.

It seems strange that a branch of the Court should have been established in Malta, centred on the Duke's official residence, San Antonio, where he and his wife, Marie of Russia (daughter of the Tsar Alexander II), lived on the lines of Buckingham Palace, if less rigidly – largely because of the young people who came to stay. Among them were the Duke's five daughters the eldest of whom, also Marie or 'Missy', four years older than David, became such a close friend that they continued to correspond long after she married Ferdinand, King of Rumania; despite the fact that she had been expected to become the wife of her cousin George, the future King George V. In the stiff circumstances of 'royal' Malta any sort of youthful romance was out of the question, and Midshipmen were less than dust beneath the feet of Missy's international clan; including Queen Victoria's youngest daughter Beatrice (1857–1944) who would marry Henry Prince of Battenburg, 'Liko', the father of Lord Louis Mounbatten.

Never was there a time when the world scene appeared more stable; dominated by an Empire of unparalleled extent and unassailable power. Yet, unnoticed by the European ruling class, their upper crust was already cracking. From traditional eggs industry was hatching new species, and some were birds of prey. They became pests on the old, farmyard economy, creating unrest which soon affected everyone's way of life, and thought. They in turn hatched out new methods, techniques, machines to do men's work; from which not even the hidebound Royal Navy could longer remain immune. Indeed, our Admiral was one of the last true sailors, for his early ships either had no engines or only enough power to assist their sails. Between *Alexandra*, fully rigged, and *Queen Elizabeth* in which he accepted the surrender of the German High Seas fleet, lay the whole gamut of change since Nelson.

Meanwhile, the body politic was also in ferment. Behind the Nineties' laughter and the last high kicks could be heard the plod of heavy footsteps: Trade Unionists trudging purposefully to branch meetings, workers marching on strike, of socialist politicians preparing to capture Wesminster; and of the New Woman 'climbing northern hills unchaperoned by a single maiden aunt'. From all this at least the junior members of the charmed circle were insulated: at home by layers of etiquette laid on like plaster bandage, abroad by the code of *comme-il-faut* regardless of location, climate, and the natives.

In the tropics one changed for dinner, stiff ('boiled') shirt and either dinner jacket or uniform. With the latter, spurs were worn though there might be no horses in the country. For instance, on a royal tour of India in 1905 Princess (later Queen) Mary was sketched in a day–coach of the special train. She wears a suffocating ensemble she might have borne for an afternoon at Ascot races. With hat and high collar, corsetted and gloved, she sits inflexible in an unpright chair while her husband reads a newspaper. Two native bearers in white 'jibbas', with E.R. for Edward Rex, nearly a foot high on the chest, squat awkwardly on the carpet.[1]

---

[1] From Guildhall Library reproduced in *The Royal House of Windsor* (Longford (E)).

Edwardian fashions are nostalgic, now, as echoes of ancestral voices, which, had anyone then listened to them, would have forecast the breakdown of the old social order. For whenever constriction becomes painful something has to give: maybe only a stay-lace but perhaps a complete rejection of the old mode. At the end of the last century the religious, political, economic and technical 'clothes' of the West, along with all outward forms and appearances, were rapidly becoming unbearable.

This is what made the First War inevitable, and, though it is still sometimes referred to as the Kaiser's doing, he was himself swept along, and away, by the wind of change. More perhaps than any other nation the Teutonic *gestalt*, adequately represented by the *Almanach de Gotha*, had to loosen up; as happens, sooner or later, with any rigid régime. The only questions then are how soon, and with how much bloodshed? A principle – if it is not an axiom – which today may be causing anxiety in many parts of the world. Yet the omens are not necessarily dire, any more than they were at the turn of the century; for the adoption of a looser style of living could have been, at least in theory, both gradual and gentle instead of sudden and ferocious. Either way it had to come, and, all unknowing, our Admiral was there at the start. He would also live to see, in the Russian Empire, an equal and opposite reaction of terrible intensity.

A week may be a long time in politics, but during the whole vacillating course of western civilisation at least one principle has remained constant amid changing circumstances – that of the seesaw. The victor of today becomes the victim of tomorrow. Were it not for a few exceptional individuals in each generation, this knock-for-knock, by which all the old empires were destroyed, must, sooner or later, bring about the disintegration of our first world-culture. These few, though they come from most dissimilar backgrounds, have in common a kind of vision. They see beyond the morbid dualism, and whether consciously or no, serve an integrating power. No easy road is theirs.

It is natural to think of David Beatty in terms of the Service, but his wider experience is, in the long run, more important. He was able to observe at first hand not only the social sickness of the Old Order in Europe and the emergence of that kind of self-determination which is another name for chaos. He watched the painful birth of anti-colonialism, and saw it grow strong enough to destroy what had been the sacred principle of nationalism based on god-fearing patriotism.

The consequence was that, despite his unique achievement, and the self-confident optimism which sustained him through such trials as few can ever encounter, he became bitterly cynical and disillusioned, not only with politics but also with people.

This is not to his discredit. For mundane characters it is enough to do a job and raise a family, but genius – and this he certainly possessed – is never content. It seeks always a greater challenge, a more severe ordeal; and so it was with David in person. He was like a mountaineer who, having reached the ultimate summit, cannot or will not return to the valley whence he came. No one can live, for long, upon a mountain top.

2

THROUGH THE MILL

Educational methods changed little, if at all, during the nineteenth century, and what changes there were occurred more because of practical considerations such as techniques than because of any weakening in the faith of God as the Great Headmaster. Having created boys as savages, he looked to his deputies to put taming before teaching. The essence of the system was moulding of character. Instruction was a secondary consideration, and only those subjects were studied which could not be of any practical use; for the hierarchy of social grades, like Service rank, depended about equally on family connections and promotion prospects.

At no stage in the educational process was a candidate encouraged to display initiative: 'theirs not to reason why'. This was particularly true of the Royal Navy. Until an officer reached Flag Rank he had no training in handling more than his ship. Even a Captain was supposed only to look after his own, and obey orders; a potentially dangerous frame of mind even when fleets were relatively slow, small, and of limited gun-range. During the Great War it was probably responsible for more lost oportunities, needless misunderstandings and pointless losses than any other single factor except defective communications.

In striving with his contemporaries and conforming to his seniors David Beatty had the advantage of a harsh childhood. If he had not been born tough, he certainly acquired toughness at a tender age. One of the first lessons he learned from his father was that in any race there can be only one winner. He would also have learned that, contrary to the Old Testament adage, the battle *is* to the strong, save in a spiritual context, such as *non vi sed arte*; and he would not be thinking about that yet. Like many before him though fewer after him, he would have been exclusively concerned with the problem of conforming to the system while secretly preserving freedom of thought and potential for initiative. The assumption of the hierarchy was that who bends not shall be broken, so the task of juniors, at best, was to bend just so far and no more; not only to avoid being broken, but in order to remain the captain of one's soul.

Consequently, acceptable characters for the quarter-deck were neither cast iron, which shatters on impact, nor tin, which is malleable; but sword-steel, forged between the hammer of discipline and the anvil of endurance. Here too David began with a certain advantage, in that in all his trials he had a staunch ally, though seldom as a physical presence. From their earliest years he and his elder brother had formed an alliance against their tyrannical father and demanding mother; and this developed as they grew to become a life-long bond of empathy. In maturity they were closer to each other than to anyone else, and at Charlie's death David was in despair, – perhaps the only occasion on record – 'we lived together, played together, rode together, fought together'.[1]

Malta was virtually British territory. Not only was our naval presence all-pervading at sea; on land it was sustained by complex ancillary services for dockyard and barracks, many of whose people brought out their families. These were quick to appreciate the sunny climate and write home about it. Although the word tourist is hardly applicable, many civilians did come out to spend agreeable months on the island; particularly those with marriagable daughters. Consequently there was a demand for sport and entertainment beyond what was required for the diversion of Servicemen (such as a pack of beagles), and when this spontaneously came into being, life became even more enjoyable, – at least for visitors. Families living there all the year round were not so happy, for winter could be dank and cold, food was dull, monotonous, and sometimes dangerous from lack of hygiene. Malta Fever particularly affected children, until the source of infection was traced to the filthy udders of the island's goats. There were no cows and almost no garden produce.

[1] Letter written to his wife from *Queen Elizabeth*.

Seagoing personnel largely escaped these rigours and ranged widely over the Mediterranean: almost an English lake, with friendly countries to the north and their Protectorates to the south. For a young naval officer there was seldom a dull day, ashore or afloat; which must have made a signal contrast to life aboard the training ship. So it is surprising to find David claiming to work more than he was obliged to. Had ambition already stirred, or was the implication an excuse for not writing home as frequently as he ought? Certainly there were fewer letters surviving from this period than from any other. There was, however, one discordant factor. It seems that, contrary to what was generally assumed, discipline tended to be harder on potential favourites than on those with no pretensions, and this applied to exams the results of which would determine seniority for ever more. It looked as though his career, like so many others, would be a slow climb and a daunting prospect. He need not have worried. Four years later, in May 1890, he was duly gazetted Sub-Lieutenant and had to acquire the various 'rigs' (orders of dress) required by Regulations. There could be as many as ten, from full dress with epaulettes and sword through decreasing formality to nondescript old clothes for dirty work. The range included Whites for summer, and though the whole gamut would not have had to be acquired all at once, becoming an Officer was, from this point of view, an expensive business. Fortunately, the Navy tailors, Gieves, were very much aware of this and gave generous credit.

By this time he had completed various courses of instruction and served in a very different ship: the humble corvette[1] *Ruby*, with little in the way of engines but a fine spread of sail. In her he learned the harsh realities of seafaring in foul weather . . . the Mediterranean can be anything but a lake in winter gales . . . but he was already clothed also in a carapace of self-assurance which he developed into what his critics called arrogance or 'side'. Already there was some reason for this. Though of youthful smoothness in appearance, the jaw was already determined as his stance. There is no doubt that he was aware, not only of his competence, but also of his good looks, and to be a 'Sub' under twenty was good going.

---

[1] *Corvette*: flush-decked warship with one tier of guns.

A couple of years later, 1892, another plum came his way, perhaps, but not necessarily, through social success. This was a special posting to the Royal Yacht for the duration of Queen Victoria's 'holiday' abroad. In fact it was more like a mourning cruise, due to her morbid preoccupation with mortality, acquired at the Prince Consort's bedside thirty-one years before, and which had been strengthened by subsequent losses. In this case there was good cause for melancholy. Her grandson, Albert Duke of Clarence, Prince of Wales and heir, therefore, to the throne, at Sandringham caught influenza from one of his sisters. Pneumonia set in. Within a week he was dead. Eddy, as he was called, was Victoria's best beloved, and she was prostrated with grief. Hence the need to escape from places and people which reminded her of death. Nor was she the only mourner. Prince George, next in line and future George V, who had recently been ill himself and was totally unprepared, took it very hard. His father was old and poorly. The notion that one day he might be Rex Imperator had never seemed likely enough to be taken seriously, and, despite what he had been through in Britannia, he was totally committed to a professional career in the Navy, without benefit of royalty. The sudden loss of his elder brother filled him not only with grief but also also with regret for his own blighted career.

He could hardly have guessed that one of the yacht's crew would be a Sub-Lieutenant Beatty, who, in that climacteric year had secret troubles of his own. For then he gained his majority, which meant that he would have to be told of his illegitimacy; supposing that his father had not earlier have felt compelled to do so. And there were now, besides Charles, two other brothers, both born in lawful wedlock.

With her grieving owner and discreet entourage the steam yacht *Osborne*[1] proceeded through the Straits of Gibraltar to the South of France, and there anchored, with attendant guardship, wherever the Queen elected to go ashore; sometimes accompanied by a white donkey to draw her bath-chair. Occasionally she would land from a ship's boat in some remote spot where she could pass unrecognised by the local people. At other times an hotel would be taken over with much protocol. Then, as the hot

[1] H.M. Yacht *Victoria and Albert* was built in 1901.

weather began, she proceeded north by train to visit her German relatives. *Osborne* returned to Portsmouth whence David took passage to the Levant and a battleship hopefully named *Trafalgar*. In the following year, 1893, he was transferred to *Camperdown*, only three months after she had rammed and sunk the flagship of Admiral Tryon with the unnecessary loss of 385 lives. Appropriately, the flagship was named *Victoria*, for she was queen of the fleet, the biggest, most up-to-date vessel in the Mediterranean. Commander Jellicoe was not only in her when she was rammed, he was in the sick bay, fever stricken. Even so, the doctor got him on deck in time to be one of the 291 who were taken off by boats from other ships in the squadron.

The reason for the high loss of life was the Admiral's order, as *Victoria* began to sink, that, although readied for rescue, boats should not be lowered. This compounded his initial error, the direct cause of the collision: an order for the two lines abreast to turn inward when everyone else could plainly see there was not enough seaway. Though *Camperdown's* Captain Markham queried the order, when it was repeated neither he nor any other Officer took evasive action. Tryon's last remark as his ship was sinking under him was, 'It was all my fault,' but that did nothing to calm the storm of scandal which was still blowing hard when Beatty joined *Camperdown* and there began his life-long friendship with Jellicoe; with whom he would serve not only in the Grand Fleet but also in China. There was another aspect of the matter which the two must have discussed, particularly because of Beatty's streak of superstition. Not only was Tryon's order completely incompatible with his record as an outstandingly good tactician and an expert in seamanship but a mystery concerns his wife's party which was being held in London. Being one of the most fashionable gatherings of the season, the Eaton Square house was filled with guests with no other thought than exchanging gossip and enjoying themselves. Suddenly, in the main reception room, some of the guests drew back to let a tall, haggard-faced figure in naval uniform pass. They were surprised to see that it was Sir George Tryon for, as far as they knew, he was supposed to be with the fleet in the Mediterranean, and certainly Lady Tryon mentioned nothing about his coming home on leave. But just as those who were making way for him began to exclaim in surprise the figure vanished. Only later came the news of the sinking of Britain's mightiest battle-ship.'[1]

To David Beatty there would not have been anything particu-larly wonderful about Tryon's reappearance in London a few hours after his body drowned off the coast of Syria. Both he and his brother Charlie inherited the Celtic aptitude for response to the unseen, and when he became an Admiral, or even before, it may have been an element in his uncanny ability to see through 'the fog of war' when others knew not where they were or what to do. Though in relation to an Admiral 'genius' may seem inappropriate, the evidence for something like it is impressive; as indeed it was with his hero, Nelson: a kind of vision seen through the mind's eye. Only when some such factor is recognised does the Admiral's amazing career become explicable in terms of character, temperament, and bloodstream.

Meanwhile, having effectively taken over Egypt, the British Government, faced with an insurrection in the Sudan, feared it might spread northward and infect Egypt with a new wave of Moslem fanaticism, as happened in 1884–1885 when General Gordon was sent out to withdraw the British garrisons but instead was cut off, and eventually cut down in Khartoum. The insult to Britannia had never been forgotten, and the emergence of another charismatic leader, such as the Mahdi of Allah had been, provided a convincing excuse for a campaign which would secure Egypt by regaining control of the Sudan, and, at the same time, revenge Gordon. The moral justification for such a move went further than that. This expedition would be a Crusade, not only against the insurgents under their Khalifa, but against Islam as the sworn enemy of Christendom, a naive over-simplification typical of those Imperial days when there were no half-tones in human relations but only allies or enemies, good or evil, white or black. Not even Gordon himself could allow that Judeo-Christianity and Islam were inspired from the same source, the ineffable One; but the Mahdi did. There need have been no sack of Khartoum, no murder of its Governor, had Gordon's noncon-formist conscience permitted him to see that when the Mahdi

[1] Alexander (M): *Phantom Britain* (Muller) 1975.

presented him with a Dervish robe it need not have been the insult for which he took it; kicking the gift away with his boot.

Of the elaborate plans as they secretly matured in London, one vital aspect concerned the Navy, for if there were a single principle of tactics which the earlier expedition had established, under General Sir Garnet Wolseley, it was that the success of ground forces depended absolutely on control of the great river. They would be moving a thousand miles and more into the African interior, and for half of that distance, north of Khartoum, the final objective, the line of communications between the army's main body and its railhead would be liable to constant harassment. What happened before on no account must even become a possibility. Revenge must be complete, and infallible, for the Sudan had been lost because, unable to keep the river open, Gordon not only became cut off from supplies, his only other link with the outside world, the telegraph line, was destroyed by enemy action. Should this happen again, no expeditionary force, regardless of size and equipment, could hope to avoid the same fate; so the key question at the War Office became, 'How can we guarantee not only freedom of passage but also command of both banks?' and the answer had to be a flotilla of armed vessels backed up by transports under their protection. Some of Gordon's boats were still afloat and Arab sails were plentiful, but the new requirement would demand specially designed vessels, sent out from England in sections to be erected at railhead. For these the Army could not be responsible, so the Navy's secondary role would be action in support of ground forces.

Rumours of this kind reached Malta, and young David saw in them a possibility of active service though his chances of selection seemed minimal. He had never been further than Alexandria, knew little about the vast area of the Sudan, and even less about the immemorial Nile; navigable two thousand miles from the sea. Ruefully he would have reflected that, since Egypt had been a British Protectorate for the past eleven years, there must be experienced officers, not necessarily in either Service, who already possessed the vital knowledge and experience which he conspicuously lacked. Then came another stroke of luck. The Commander of *Trafalgar* was Stanley Colville, later Admiral, who had served on the Nile under General Wolseley in attempting, too late, to relieve Khartoum; and this Beatty must have known for they had served together in the Royal Yacht. It was thus natural for Kitchener to nominate Colville, and for the latter to put forward Beatty's name. Both would be seconded to the Egyptian Government, and the boats at their disposal would wear, not the White Ensign but the Star and Crescent.

Looking back, it is not difficult to see why Lieutenant Beatty was given his first command in such unusual circumstances. The type Kitchener needed was not that of the old sea-dog, set in his ways, but the adventurous young officer, full of dash and daring. No doubt David's record in this respect was already indicative of great things to come, for he was accepted. He and Colville proceeded to Cairo, were passed to Army Command and briefed by the Commander-in-Chief,[1] with two other naval officers and one Marine. This curious circumstance of naval personnel being responsible, though so junior, direct to the General commanding a large and complex force, would not at first sight seem promising. That in practice it worked well says much for both poles of the command, particularly in that Kitchener, instead of taking refuge in his headquarters, made a point of cultivating the personal friendship of his sailors.

The advance began on 13th September 1898, too soon for the new boats to be ready, so Colville and Beatty found themselves in far less powerful vessels, which nevertheless would give a good account of themselves. Superiority on the river was rapidly established, and with the arrival of the new boats, supremacy. Considering the tremendous difficulties of handling anything bigger than a picket-boat, it was an extraordinary achievement; for which the size and weight of them speak clearly:- Length 120 ft., Armament 12 pounders, 6 pounders, maxims. Equipment: ammunition hoists, steam winches, searchlights.

It seems a lot of iron and steel to handle among the treacherous currents and shoals, always unpredictable, and often dangerous; the more so since the new boats drew less than four feet of water and were dependent on wood for fuel, seldom reliable, often in short supply.

The essence of seamanship is manoeuvre, but on a river, though it be as big as the Amazon, there is hardly any such thing.

[1] For General Kitchener a new rank was created in deference to Egyptian opinion: *Sirdar*.

Because of the risk of going aground a boat is 'canalised', often in the tight sense that she cannot even go about, in which respect the Nile varied widely but was always more or less dangerous, even when there was no enemy presence and timber could be found to feed the boilers. For hundreds of miles there were no trees at all: only desert or the sea of reeds called *sudd*. Fuel was therefore a constant anxiety.

Of this and other difficulties there is no hint in David's letters, and at this time he was a fairly regular correspondent, having time on his hands between the phases of active operations. Indeed, his light touch is such that he might have been describing a series of picnics. This was not the simple British affectation of 'emphasis by understatement'. There was an element of cynicism such that, if one did not know the other side of his character, he might be suspected of callousness, indifference to suffering. For instance, he records 'the butcher's bill' for 'a day's entertainment'. Later, on going ashore after a riverside town had been shelled from the Nile, then sacked by troops, 'A City of the Dead, just as they fell, including women and children in every stage of decay.'

Despite such horrors he takes great pride in Army pageantry, as, when ashore in support of an attack, he noted the magnificent spectacle of infantry advancing in close order preceded by their music. As an instance of the variety of missions with which he was concerned, on this occasion he commanded a naval detachment with a battery of Congreve rockets. First used against the Taiping rebels, these were not lethal weapons, having no warheads. They were intended to create panic and frighten horses, in which on a flat trajectory, they succeeded; but it is odd in retrospect that no one seems to have developed the rocket principle for warfare until nearly fifty years later.

To advance in close order was not the folly it would be in modern times, for against the Dervish horde was ranged an immense superiority of material which more than compensated for their numerical strength. Their small arms were few and antique, so the principal weapons were iron swords and spears. The only personal protection was afforded by shields of ox-hide, so they were completely vulnerable to rifle fire. They possessed a few field-pieces, but these were of little use unless they had a compact target. As the Army was by no means anxious to provide that sort of thing the enemy artillery, such as it was, concentrated on the gunboats wherever they could be found; and in this were often effective.

Thanks to meticulous preparation and efficient organisation, the advance, if slow, proceeded according to plan, despite determined harassment from both banks of the Nile. The aim was to push the enemy southward without a major battle, until he had concentrated the majority of forces available to him. For the opposite reason to Kitchener's, who relied on superior fire-power from numerical inferiority, the enemy's plan was similar. His intention was to draw the invaders deeper and deeper into the Sudan while concentrating an overwhelming force, firearms notwithstanding; made up of untrained fellaheen from a widely scattered population, loosely grouped on a temporary basis: not much of an army, more of a horde.

Inexorably the columns advanced, leaving at intervals detachments to protect the line of communications from raiders. For these also – at least in the forward areas – the gunboats were in part responsible. That they could be spared was due to the Army taking over every Arab craft they could find, reinforced by several tourist steamers, owned by Thomas Cook, which, because of their several decks, were ideal transports though vulnerable to rifle-fire. Additional gunboats were put together from sections at the railhead at Kosheh, but were not ready in time when the Sirdar decided to push further on. So Beatty's first boat was one of the original flotilla, part of the pre-war establishment, called *Abu Klea*. Later, the new *Fateh* caught up with him and he transferred to her, but not before he twice nearly lost his life. On the first occasion he heaved a live shell overboard. On the second, having capsized in a cataract, he claimed to have gone down six times, and two of his crew were drowned.

As if gauntlet-running on the river between enemy batteries were not enough to satisfy his zest for danger, he frequently operated ashore in support of troops. He even acquired a horse, no easy matter, for no one would be likely to lend his charger to another officer, let alone to a sailor. Taking the rough with the smooth, – for there were frequent periods when nothing much was happening – this was the kind of life he needed. He was for the first time a long, long way from home with its threatened complications. Perhaps that is why, despite the gory scenes he had to witness, his letters are lighthearted. They read as though from a youth abroad after an oppressive childhood, revelling in man's estate and freedom from family ties.

The railhead was advanced to Berber, from which the last phase of the expedition began; still according to plan but with Kitchener's force so greatly outnumbered that, but for the rifleman's ability to kill at a distance, it must have ended in defeat; as succinctly recorded in Beatty's journal, which he wrote up like a diary. 'The first onslaught of the enemy attack (at Omdurman) was beaten off with enormous losses. The endless columns of warriors led by mounted Emirs moving steadily on. It was a pitiable sight to see the effect of our fire all along the line. They were simply mown down, and in very few parts of the line did they approach nearer than 600 yards.'

Other observers confirm that the enemy never succeeded in getting close enough to do any serious damage, but an Army Officer would query that accurate rifle fire was feasible at 600 yards, a distance which, even on a range, would make it difficult for a marksman to hit a human figure, although standing still. Laconically, David sums up:- 'Of 80,000 Dervish, 10,883 were killed in the course of a few hours.' One tends to think of the colonial campaigns in the last century as little more than skirmishing, but those figures are comparable with battles on the Western Front in the war of 1914–1918; yet they occured at the very end of a precarious line of communication of unprecedented length. As G. W. Steevens, a war correspondent, dramatised the slaughter, 'No white troops would have faced that torrent of death for five minutes. It was not a battle but an execution. Within an hour or two there were ten thousand bodies lying out there. Kitchener's casualties were about 400.'

Before the clash of arms began, when the mixed British, Egyptian and Sudanese force, which was 'K's' unique command, was calmly watching the approach of the enemy horde, 'as though the very sands were moving', the Staff were taking luncheon in the open when a young fellow cantered up in a cloud of dust and announced there was a battle in progress. They ignored him and went on eating. The horseman was Winston Churchill. The anecdote has become famous to the point where credulity is strained, but the Sirdar's Intelligence Officer, subsequently

General Wingate though then only a Major, described it in detail for my benefit. That was in Brussels, when he was over ninety. He also recalled that Churchill was at the time attached to the 21st Lancers, which made a gallant but ineffectual charge, thereby breaking the sacrosanct 'principle of war' known as 'economy of force'; in this case meaning it were folly to close the enemy when they can be dealt with at a distance.

Wingate also recalled that the Lancers were supported by a white gunboat, mentioned by Churchill as under Beatty's command. Since *Fateh* and her sisters had dark hulls, often covered with sheet iron, the white boat was probably *Ramases*, outstanding not only for her colour but also for her height. One suspects that Beatty may have acquired her, temporarily, to add panache to this very special occasion: a gesture quite typical of him. Perhaps that is one reason why he was invited to their Mess, where he met Churchill, a significant coincidence and the start of their long friendship. Indeed, there was a strong personal reason why Churchill should wish to meet Beatty. He knew about the scandal of Edith's divorce, for he recorded in *World Crisis* that the Admiral's father 'was much talked about when I first joined (the 4th Hussars)'. So 'the Captain' was still remembered, and probably still is. Regiments have long memories.

Except for mopping up, the battle at Omdurman ended the River War and avenged General Gordon. It also rendered inevitable British occupation of the Sudan, which became 'Anglo-Egyptian'. So ended David's first tour of duty on active service, during which he was promoted Commander over the heads of 395 contenders with longer service records. As Lieutenants they were required to put in twelve and a half years. Beatty came up in half that time: by no means the last occasion when he received preferment of an unusual, if not unique, character; a circumstance which in later years provided ammunition for his enemies. In the eye of history most of their rounds were blanks, for now that the facts are marshalled it were not only uncharitable but unreasonable to claim, that on any occasion, his promotion was achieved otherwise than on merit. Back to the eighteenth century and beyond, 'interest', – being a euphemism for influence in high places, – was courted and accepted by the Navy as a legitimate advantage. Admiral Lord Rodney is a case in point, but it may be that, of all his illustrious predecessors, David Beatty, despite a poor start, acquired more 'interest' than any of them. Of course it advantaged him, but it did not secure him unearned promotion.

Being entitled to long leave, he went home towards the end of 1893, having acquired, in addition to the D.S.O., the Khartoum medal and another citation in Despatches. It could not have been much of a homecoming, for his father, at fifty-four, had succeeded to Borodale in 1881 though he still ran his stables at The Mount, near Rugby, where Edith, an alcoholic, died. He himself was a heavy drinker and already alienated from his two elder boys by what, to put it mildly, would now be called 'the generation gap'.

David brought with him to Borodale a number of relics to add to the collection already hanging on the walls of the inner hall, lit only by a long skylight. There were spears with leaf-shaped blades of crude iron nine inches long and four broad, two-handed swords in scabbards of ill-dressed leather, the heavy cotton jacket called *jibba*, patched with bright colours, worn by Dervishes in battle, and, in pride of place, a white pith-helmet with a bullet-hole fore and aft from a shot which must have been within an inch of the head.

He did not stay long, for the life-style of Wexford's 'county' families was alien to him, and his father was under considerable strain, since the Moat, which had at one time about forty 'chasers in training,–steeplechasing being the amateur's sport as distinct from professional jockeys of the 'flat' – could not be managed from Ireland and had to be disposed of. Fortunately, it was on a lease. So he went to stay with Charles at Newmarket, as yet unmarried, where he could meet the right people to provide him with a season's hunting of a quality which the 'trappy' country around Borodale could not match; and also accommodate his otherwise homeless person in aristocratic houses which, because of his heroic reputation, would be only too glad to receive him. Also he had marriage in mind, or at least an intimate relationship which would endure; for outside the Service he had few friends, and, since Malta, hardly any female acquaintance.

Then, one day out hunting he saw, beside a field-gate, a vision which might have been the projection of a dream wrought out of lonely and perilous nights: a young woman on a side-saddle, veiled as required when wearing a top hat, yet instantly appealing.

She turned out to be Ethel Field, only child of Marshall Field, founder of a fortune based on a Chicago store. She was about David's height, slim and graceful with a long neck, eloquent eyes, high cheekbones and dark hair. Perhaps more important even than her looks, or her expectations, she went like the wind to hounds.

The combination was too much for David after his long exile from society. After the impact of love at first sight the empathy between them strengthened till both believed they were 'made for each other' and their love would endure for life. With qualifications it did so endure; but there was from the start an element of mutual infatuation which is no surrogate for true love. They needed imperatively to possess one another, and, as Admiral Chalmers remarks, 'it was foreign to his nature to be kept waiting'. Quite so, but the headlong chase is seldom without checks. Marry they did, and family history repeated itself.

Another of our Admirals's characteristics was to back apparently spontaneous decisions with cold, clear expediency. In relation to Ethel Tree, as she then was, with one child called Ronald, this must have been as evident from the start as his genuine need for her, – in more senses than one. As a second son, with no home and no patrimony, David would not have been human had he failed to recognise in his heiress a match which would be expedient. Already he had achieved enough fame to assure his career. As Edith used to claim to her friends, 'One day England will ring with his name'. None the less he would be permanently hard up unless substantial funds could be aquired from somewhere outside his own family. Nearly all naval officers had private incomes, often large, for they were expected to live sociable lives when ashore and go in for expensive sports such as polo. By contrast, a Captain at the turn of the century was paid only £600 a year.

This meant that even if David Beatty had the temperament to live modestly he would have had difficulty in making ends meet, but he demanded an expensive life-style and the kind of company which goes with it.

He would naturally have talked this over with Charles at Bedford Cottage and been told that nothing could be expected from their father now that Borodale had begun its long decline and the English property,–chiefly the Moat–had been wound up. There was no profit from it either, for the horses belonged to other people. Nor could Charles lend a helping hand, for though he was a successful trainer with a dozen or more race-horses in his stables, both brothers knew, only too well, how precarious is a run of luck. Add that Charles also intended to marry, and therefore needed to acquired some capital rather than borrow against his inheritance of the Irish estates. Of the other brothers, Vandy was in much the same position except that he had no expectations, and George was out of reach in India.

Such a discussion could have been embarassing, because Charles differed from David radically in his attitude to money, subscribing to the view that no gentleman should give it a thought. Indeed, when first he proposed to Lu, my mother-to-be, and she said she could not accept him unless she knew his financial standing, he claimed he really had no idea how he stood, and suggested that she ask the Bank. 'They know about such things'. As the daughter of a banking family, Beck of Shrewsbury, which became one of the roots of Lloyds, she had no hesitation, and the result was satisfactory. Even so, they did not marry until 1905, nor was I born until five years later.

David, on the other hand was usually careful about money. In his early career he had to be, and being careful could lead to being mean. At the same time he was by no means averse to money-making for its own sake, not sharing his brother's romantic notion about gentlemen, in theory, being above the sordid pursuit of lucre. All of which brought back the main issue, the need for David to *marry* money. Surely that would give him the best of both worlds, and love also? Charles could hardly disagree, though Lu's portion from her uncle, Arthur Beck, would be very modest indeed compared to Ethel's dollars.

David must have left Newmarket with his mind made up. Nor would he have hesitated to press on because the lady happened to have a husband already. What had been good enough for his father was good enough for him. If, under far more difficult circumstances, 'the Old Master' had been able to corral Edith, when at least the outward moral code was far more strict, it should be relatively easy to detach Ethel from Arthur Tree. Americans were supposed to be much more lax in such matters than the British.

What could hardly have occurred to him, but would have struck a note of caution if it had, was that Ethel was totally unlike Edith. Far from being a homebody, fiercely possessive in the narrow pound of one man, one home, she was very sophisticated, much travelled, and free ranging in her affections. If she allowed 'Jack', as she called him, – though no one else dared so to do – to corral her, it would be because she felt confident he could not keep her in. That, however, as yet he was not to know. He would find out later, the hard way.

3

CHINA AND
ROMANCE (1898–1900)

As one of the few naval officers to have seen active service, and the only one to have been through the whole of Kitchener's campaign, Commander Beatty was an obvious choice for the British contingent of an international force sent, in 1899, to protect western nationals in northern China from secret military organisations. They were known as Boxers because they originated under cover of gymnastic and boxing clubs of which the first was called the Fists of Public Harmony. Despite the Imperial Government's declared policy of encouraging Westernisation in terms of progress it encouraged the irregular forces to the point where they were as well trained and equipped as the Army, from which they were virtually indistinguishable.

Following the murder of hundreds of missionaries and their converts, all foreigners and their property were at risk, culminating in the murder of the German Minister. Installations of all kinds, including railways, were subject to widespread sabotage and not even diplomatic enclaves were safe from molestation. The Powers had to intervene lest they be thrown out of the whole country, with its huge potential for western trade, and the loss of many lives.

The initial move was to create a mixed force out of separate detachments sent to protect American, British, German, Japanese and Russian footholds. Its first task was to force the passage of the Pei-Ho river leading to Tientsin, capital of Hopeh Province, and thence to Peking; a distance of about a hundred miles in a straight line but many more by water or rail.

Although before leaving England Beatty could not have

known of the plan of campaign, the idea of again penetrating deep into unknown and hostile territory in the course of another River War must have fired his imagination. At last he would be going to China Station, where, had it not been for his mother's appeal to Lord Beresford, he would have served years before, in a very humble capacity; missing Malta, the Nile, promotion and his heiress. As Commander of the capital ship *Barfleur* he had great executive responsibility and would have been tied down by routine were it not that his Captain was an old friend and comrade of the Nile, Stanley Colville. Having already shared so many adventures, he was happy to accede to Beatty's request that he be allowed to command a detachment of forty Marines for the drive up-river towards Tientsin, an operation only superficially on the lines of the Nile advance; for the mixed force, necessarily, lacked adequate organisation, centralised control and integrated training.

Until landings had been successful there was no means of knowing what opposition, if any, would be encountered, and at the first attempt the Marines were met by fire from shore batteries, which compelled them to retire, pending reduction of the forts to rubble. The Chinese fought gallantly against vastly superior armament, leaving most of their guns' crews dead. If there were substantial supporting forces in the area the chances of getting to Tientsin must be slim indeed, unless the Provincial Government were prepared to intervene. Having no boats at their disposal, the two hundred Marines which formed an advance guard had to function as auxiliary infantry constituting the core of a polyglot 'army' of doubtful fighting quality. They were fortunate not to encounter serious opposition until they reached Tientsin and, having entered the city, were besieged; as no doubt had been intended by the enemy: a trap. Jellicoe was there, and senior to Beatty, so it must have been his decision to send the gallant two hundred on what can only be described as a desperate mission: attack and silence the enemy guns which were knocking the town to bits.

Although twice wounded, in his left hand and arm, Beatty continued to lead his men towards the guns until checked by small-arms fire. Since it was vital to the defence to avoid unnecessary casualties, the Marines were halted where there was some cover, and before they retired he noticed a casualty out in the open, unable to stand. Knowing that, with only one arm he could not lift the man, and no doubt realising what the Boxers were likely to do to him if taken alive, Beatty hailed a fellow who had taken cover behind a near-by rock. Under heavy fire the two of them managed to bring the casualty to safety as the whole force began to withdraw, and soon gained the relative safety of the town's permanent defences, manned by Chinese. Only then did he report to the hospital, where he was detained and joined by John Jellicoe, who had also been wounded. Thus by a strange chance two men who would successively command the greatest of all fleets became as it were, blood brothers as a result of the same action. And the bond held, life-long; for Beatty would write, following a reunion after the Great War, 'we were like brothers'.

Tientsin was relieved before the enemy could take it by assault, and Beatty went back to his ship to await passage home. It soon came, and while he was still at sea the greater siege, of the Peking Legations, was also lifted and the Rising petered out.[1] He was again mentioned in Despatches and said to be in the running for a Victoria Cross on account of his valour in aid of the casualty, or, failing that, a bar to his D.S.O. Instead he would be promoted Captain. There was only one blot on his seascape, – Ethel Tree.

Even during the campaign word had reached him that she had taken up with another man, whose identity was quite widely known because he belonged to a distinguished family. So that was why she had stopped writing to him! Seemingly, their relationship was at an end and the rosy future nothing but wishful thinking. Her behaviour was unforgivable, and since there was no formal engagement he could not even have the satisfaction of seeking out her paramour to see him off. It was ever 'all or none' with David Beatty, as with his father before him. Ethel had gone, taking with her his devotion. Better than bickering over half a loaf!

On landing, a telegram and a letter awaited him, both from Ethel. She had heard about him being wounded and reacted as would any caring woman, but he took it as another insult and

---

[1] The Empress Tzu Hsi secretly supported the Boxers, but her army was either uncommitted or hostile to them. Jung Lu, commander of the Peking area armies, sent presents to the legations while the siege was on.

refused to respond until, after an operation in a London nursing home, he could no longer repress his feelings and wrote to her on 15th September 1900:—

> *'I landed from China with my heart full of rage, and swore I did not care if ever I saw you again, or if I were killed or not. And now I have arrived with the firm determination not to see you at all in my own mind . . . Unfortunately I shall go on loving you to the bitter end . . . To me always a Queen, if not always mine.*
> *Good-bye,*
>
> *Jack (The Sailor)'*

Even that was not the end of their association, for with the start of foxhunting in November they were together again in circumstances which were sufficiently discreet to prevent a fresh round of gossip, whether about David or his rival; who was no longer in the running, though he would reappear, – or someone like him – years later. Before the year ended there was a mutual decision to marry, subject to parental approval as a matter of form. At first Marshall Field rejected the idea of his daughter marrying an impecunious naval officer, but came round when she explained the heroic nature of his career, his unique promotion, and the 'interest' he enjoyed in high places.

David's father, 'the Captain', took the threat of the alliance very differently, as well he might considering the similarity between it and his own imbroglio with Edith. Ethel was a conspicuous figure, and not only because of her wealth. If something went wrong there would be no chance of covering-up as he had succeeded in doing with Edith when they started their family. No doubt his 'sailor son' as the Captain fondly called him, was ready for this and prepared to defy his father if need be. On his own account this may well have happened, for he wrote, 'The old man fell flat on his back in a fit'. An illuminating incident, and one which provides a clue to much besides the engagement. Whatever the details, there was, after this confrontation, an increasing gap between David and his father.

Of course the informal engagement still had to be kept secret, for Arthur Tree stood in the way. It was in these anxious circumstances that David consulted a fortune-teller, Mrs Roberts, who foretold such a brilliant fortune, for them both, that he determined to press on, regardless.

Had he been more cautious he might have been put off, if only temporarily, by the character of her father, Marshall Field, 1834–1906, described in the *Dictionary of American Biography* as, 'Merchant and travelling salesman'. He prospered well enough to found perhaps the first 'one price' store, which made him a fortune to rival his successors, Woolworths, whose motto used to be 'Nothing over Sixpence'. Besides Ethel he had two sons by his first wife, Nannie Scott, but no children by his second, Delia Spencer Canton, whom he married in 1905.

The Trust he created for Ethel, on or before her first marriage, might not have been irrevocable. On her father's death, which occurred only five years after she married David Beatty, it could have been modified or annulled by his Will; which was singular in that it bypassed his sons in favour of two grandsons; with the proviso that they could not touch the bulk of the capital until thirty-nine years after the testator's death. This kind of Will was subsequently made illegal by the State of Illinois because its aim was to increase capital.

In the event, Ethel continued to enjoy a very large income for life, though the Depression may have reduced it somewhat; but, as usual, David was taking chances. She might have inherited her father's mercenary temperament, or contrariwise, her income might abruptly cease, or be drastically reduced. Meanwhile, he had other, more pressing matters to think about, particularly his health; for it seemed on the cards that he might never again be fit for active service.

Despite further operations to regenerate a severed nerve, his bad arm prevented him from returning to duty, but it did not stop him riding, and, as they saw more of each other, matters soon came to the point where definite action had to be taken. Clearly the first step was for Ethel to desert her husband, and this she set about doing in the same ruthless manner adopted by Edith; the only difference being that Ethel was by no means content to wait upon Tree's initiative over a divorce. She would compel it.

If Tree cited a co-respondent other than Beatty it might cause him to reject her, this time permanently. If on the other hand he were cited, supposing there were legal grounds for it; then whether they married or no his reputation would be impugned and his career might be blighted. It was Arthur Tree who solved the problem generously and secretly. He went back to America and quickly obtained a divorce on no grounds other than desertion. He took with him this letter:-

Feby 15 1901

'Dear Arthur,
I have thought over your suggestion that we should
live together again, and I can never consent to it. There is no use
discussing our differences. I shall never live with you again.

Yours truly,

Ethel F. Tree.'

Judgement was delivered on 9th May and filed the same day. It is amazing that the papers crossed the Atlantic, were cleared for validity in London, and were the basis of Ethel's remarriage within a month. The whole sequence of events, from her semi-detached relationship with David to her desertion of Arthur Tree was extraordinary enough. That, having been involved with someone else while David was fighting in China, – news which nearly caused him to reject her utterly – they could be reconciled and married in a matter of months says as much for the celerity of the proceedings as it does for their impatience. What a different story the Admiral's would have been had William Chaine acted as promptly as did Arthur Tree!

Another factor which links Ethel with Edith is the risk they both took that the divorce would not go through. With the latter, the question was whether Chaine would bring himself to take such a shaming step; for it was usual in those days for the husband to give his wife cause to divorce him. With the former, from the day she deserted Tree there must have been doubts as to whether an American divorce would be accepted in English law, bearing in mind that both parties were there resident. Legal opinion, however, is unequivocal:—

'It seems clear that, at the relevant time, English law would have recognised the American divorce decree provided that the decree was effective under the laws of America and that at the date of the commencement of the proceedings in America either of the parties was habitually resident in America or a national of America or both parties were domiciled there. It seems clear from the papers that both these conditions were fulfilled'.[1]

[1] Extract from a legal opinion dated 10 May 1979.

To satisfy the Court that at least two years had passed between her desertion and its judgement she could have left Tree at any time between March 1899 and May of the following year. It seems virtually certain, therefore, that first she accepted David's promise of marriage, then saw him off to China, in the April of '99, and abandoned Arthur Tree not later than the following month. Such a plan is entirely in keeping with her character as it developed, and suggests that, finding life on her own extremely dull, she acquired a playmate to pass the time until David's return. She could hardly have imagined that, in the middle of a war at the other end of the Earth, news of this development would have reached him. When he stopped writing to her she would quite properly have assumed that communications had broken down; so that was why she was so enthusiastic when he turned up, safe but not quite sound.

If such an interpretation of her actions seems harsh, it is less so in the light shed by her son, Ronald, when adult. He felt obliged to comment on these matters in his book *When the Moon was High* (1975). 'Divorce', he wrote, 'crushed my father's spirit'. And it was so. Not so much because of legal problems as because Ethel took it out on him in selfish and cruel ways: not least because she withdrew her financial support, without which he could not hope to maintain the life-style to which they were accustomed in a 'pseudo-Elizabethan style mansion' which Ethel had built around 'a small country house'. The taste is typical of her tendency to go to extremes. The mansion, of course, had to have a Minstrel's Gallery.

Arthur Tree could have stayed in America after the divorce but elected to return to Britain because he felt more at home in the Shires than in Chicago's smart and ultra rich circle to which both the Fields and the Trees belonged. When, many years later, the grown-up Ronald went over to see his grandfather he too felt Chicago inimical . . . 'The vast house. The impression of wealth was like weight'.

It is important that to win her divorce Ethel had to lose her only surviving child, for, despite the Court's order, she made every effort to get him back and turn him against his father, whom he adored. Arthur Tree died when the boy was thirteen, during school holidays. Knowing he was seriously ill, Ethel sent a stranger to take Ronald away, who was resolutely told that his duty was with his father, who died next day. Then Ethel herself appeared, on the same heartless mission; to be defied. In his book Ronald admits he could never forget nor forgive this incident, and the breach between them never healed although he was frequently her guest when, in maturity, he became a close friend of the Admiral's.

Such views are the more impressive because, as indicated by the title, – referring of course to German bombing 'when the moon was high' – Ronald is largely concerned with later history when he lent his large country house, Ditchley, only a few miles from Dingley,[1] to Churchill for secret weekends. By then Ronald was a unique high-level link between Britain and the United States. Such a man would not have mentioned the sad rift with his mother had he not felt compelled to do so, and he is the last person to speak ill of anyone; so when he refers to her as 'selfish and wilful' it is probably an understatement, and it tallies with what I knew of her. A grasping hedonism, self defeating, was the mainspring of her life, and though the Admiral was important to her, it was largely for that reason. He alone could satisfy her self-importance, which was hidden from almost everyone else because she had learned in her American childhood not only how to put her best face forward but also how to make the most of its effect. To which end she cultivated an impressive presence, when indicated, and at other times a cheerful, lighthearted manner which was at least disarming, at best charming.

She never quite lost traces of a Chicago accent, particularly in moments of stress, and it may occasionally have been something of a handicap; though in general the impression she made was that of an enviable lady of uncommonly good looks and great wealth who, in that era of pre-war ostentation with which the reign of Edward VII is still associated, would be the more sought after for being lavish. With it all, and an unladylike habit of shouting for people, particularly her husband, on a piercing note, – 'J-aaack!', she could also be kind, sympathetic, caring and even generous. These heartfelt qualities were particularly appreciated when Lu, my mother, was widowed for the second time, in 1917, aged forty-eight. More than anything Lu needed someone on whom she could rely in the grey twilight which lay ahead. There Ethel was at her best.

[1] Where Ethel died, in 1931.

The tangled web is now in focus. Edith and David the Captain, Ethel and David the Admiral were caught in it, for life, under similar circumstances. The older couple had to cover up the fact that their two first boys were bastards, and David had to take the risk that, even so late in the day, the secret might come out. If that happened it would have undermined his marriage by giving Ethel more power over him; and though he could hardly be held responsible, it might prove a professional handicap because of his 'interest' among the great. Also caught in the web, if in a different sector of it, was the unfortunate Arthur Tree. Though he had nothing on his conscience, unlike the two Davids and their wives, all four may be said to have married under flase pretences. Though Ethel did not have to conceal her status as a divorcée, her bridegroom was at fault in failing to disclose the inadvertence of his birth. Should she find out she might claim that, had he owned up, she would not have accepted him.

Although, unless Charles died without issue, none of the family property would come to David, even if he were legitimate, it remains true that had his father's later sons found out they could have dispossessed him, or, of course, my father. It is no light matter to inherit an ancestral home and live there with the feeling that any day the roof may be lifted off. All this because of 'the dash of a cavalry-man' and the passionate impatience of a strong-minded, married, woman. Of the Admiral's father it may be apt to quote from Lord Tennyson's Idyls of the King[1] concerning Sir Lancelot of the Lake and his guilty love for the Queen:—

'   . . . but now the shackles of an old love
        straighten'd him,
     His honour rooted in dishonour stood,
     And faith unfaithful kept him falsely true.'

So it came about that Ethel's wedding was also to one who was 'straighten'd' by an old love. Both were held in secret at an unlikely venue with strangers for witnesses. The addresses given were peculiar and of the honeymoon nothing is known. On neither occasion were there any representatives of either family. Now, on 22nd May 1901 at the Register Office, St George,

[1] Lancelot and Elaine.

Hanover Square,[1] London, none of Ethel's kin wished to be present. Charles was in South Africa. Lu could have attended but did not. The third brother, Vandy, was also in South Africa and the last, George, in India. The only sister, 'Trot' might have been able to attend, but apparently did not. The particulars from a Certified Copy of the Marriage Certificate are as follows:—

> David Beatty age 30, Batchelor, Captain Royal Navy,
> of 128 Piccadilly. Of independent means.
> Father's name David Longfield Beatty. Of independent means.

> Ethel Field Tree, formerly Ethel Field, age 27, the divorced
> wife of Arthur Magie-Tree.
> Of Fleming's Hotel, Half Moon Street.
> Father's name Marshall Field, of independent means.

> Witnesses: Fred Spinola, Arthur Boyd.

It seems odd that David was not staying with friends for the traditional party. It is more odd that Ethel should have gone to a hotel. One can only conclude that both sought concealment, and why should they unless there was something to hide? And of course there was; in fact several things. Though it was known that Ethel had left Arthur Tree, and if she were to be divorced the betting might have made Beatty favourite for the next Marriage Stakes, the hunting and racing set could not have known about the divorce, still less that she was already free to remarry. This in itself is reason enough for a secret wedding, but it cannot be the whole explanation of why it was thought necessary to be so circumspect in a moral climate much more liberal than it had been in Edith's day.

[1] Not located near Hanover Lodge.

4
CAPTAIN COURAGEOUS

As foxhunting ends in May when the London Season begins, Ethel and David had the best of both worlds during their honeymoon, and after it could dovetail their interests. While David played polo or cricket, Ethel would welcome attendance at such events because one met the right people, as one also did at race meetings; though it sometimes irritated him that she was obsessively concerned to be 'the best dressed woman there'. This was not easily achieved, for, at the turn of the century, fashion required every part of the body to be covered, even the face, most of it so draped that it is a wonder, looking back, how able-bodied ladies were.

The Beattys were everywhere welcome, for themselves and not because of his fame or her fortune; and what he most appreciated was having, for the first time since childhood, a home of his own, even if it did belong to 'Tata' as he called her. Hanover Lodge was a solid, square, white, Georgian-type house off Regents Park, a modest establishment compared to its successors yet adequate for the entertaining Ethel so much enjoyed; particularly now that she could introduce 'Jack' to her own circle: the American connection.

One thing which etiquette demanded of her but she had to avoid was to pay her formal respects to David's father at Borodale. He was pretty far gone though he had married again after Edith's death, and David's stepmother, the redoubtable 'Mouse', whom he had never met, was unlikely to approve either of the match or of an American bride. Even without that difficulty it would be taking an unjustifiable risk to receive Ethel, supposing she were willing to come, lest the Old Man should inadvertently say something about the family which would cause acute embarrassment.

So the newlyweds had Spring and Summer to themselves, enjoying the foretaste of that good fortune which Mrs Roberts had seen in her crystal ball. Both still occasionally consulted her. Only much later, when Ethel took up spiritualist mediums, did David forego such oracles. Meanwhile Ethel's temperament began to show its underlying instability, perhaps an unconscious reaction to her harsh treatment of poor Arthur Tree. Forcing him to divorce her, losing her only surviving child and then turning him against her out of cruel tactlessness – to put it mildly – would have been enough to upset almost anyone. Whatever the cause, she had the first of many mental crises. David himself used the word 'breakdown', but he could hardly have envisaged that similar incidents would recur, at intervals, for thirty years, during which he acquired an almost saintly patience to curb his volcanic Celtic temperament. This may not have been so difficult as at first may seem, for the exigencies of high command also called for the suppression of personal feelings in the interests of discipline, the root of which is, of course, *self*-discipline.

Beneath that armour he was very like his brother Charles in having swift angry reflexes, not always suppressed. It was well recognized that the Admiral's bite was worse than his bark; but the bark could be bad enough. Charles would often overreact to some trivial matter, as some detail wrong with a horse's turnout. On more than one occasion he damned the groom into heaps, sacked him on the spot, and threw after him all the money he had in his pockets. Next morning the man would be at work as usual and nothing more would be said. In short, they had an unusual intensity of temperament, which could be controlled by an effort of will; but that effort was not made unless a grave situation arose.

In at least one other respect they were much alike. Neither could claim to be a great lover. The moral climate of their childhood had been stifling, and it continued into adolescence. Even when repression had become effective, relief from erotic tension was either sinful or a duty without joy, and both were subject to a rigid taboo. Is it surprising therefore that five years elapsed between the marriage of my parents and my birth, four years between Ethel's remarriage and the arrival of her elder son, four years more before the younger appeared?

David's formidable self-control in battle owed a lot to this more subtle discipline, further strengthened by the necessity for continence at sea. Later, as a national hero, he could never risk becoming involved in scandal. Perhaps that is a principal reason why he was such a prolific letter writer, especially to attractive women.

Such an attitude to profane love, as churchmen preferred to call a sexual relationship, persisted until after the Second World War, if in a milder form. America, however, had always been more relaxed, so Ethel's girlhood did not come under the same inhibiting influence as David's boyhood. It is no surprise, therefore, to find her relatively free from inhibitions, or indeed scruples. By the time she acquired 'Jack' she was adept at getting anything, or anyone, she wanted. At its best this trait helped several young men, usually artists, whom she took under her wing until they were successful. If they were not, she dropped them as casually as she had adopted them in the first place. In this context, taken as a whole, it is not surprising that even the first year they spent together was not all plain sailing. If it had been, why did David not play out the full length of his leave?

He went back to sea on 2nd June, 1902, five months short of his entitlement. If this was not because he had become bored with the social round, following in Ethel's wake, it may have been because he was running short of money and was, as yet, reluctant to be dependent on her. His ship was the cruiser *Juno*, and his position – another preferment, second-in-command. That he soon found himself back in Malta of happy memories must have been anything but disagreeable, till Ethel went into another depression. Fortunately it did not last long. No doubt she was resentful at being left behind as though she were an ordinary wife; but there was now so much for her to live for that she displayed unusual initiative in setting out for Malta, alone; and there rented the Capua Palace, no less, which soon became a rendezvous for the island's rank and fashion.

This agreeable routine had been shaken, but not interrupted, when David's mother died, in Cheshire, at his father's place, The Moat, near Rugby, and soon afterwards 'the Captain' withdrew to Borodale where he became something of a recluse. He died in 1904 and there are several versions of the manner of it. According to one he drank a bottle of brandy and had a heart attack. Another avers that he was bedridden and speechless for months before he abruptly sat up one day to announce, 'Edith, I'm coming to you', and fell back dead. The truth is probably somewhere in between, for he had been markedly eccentric, and a heavy drinker, for years while he neglected Borodale. And now it was too late to pull the estate back into good heart, so the mortgages were piling up, with other debts which Charles was faced with when he succeeded to the entail. It must have been with relief that David learned the inheritance had passed unchallenged, but both brothers would have been apprehensive lest somebody should check, perhaps only out of curiosity, the relevant marriage and birth certificates.

This worry must have been very much in David's mind when, in February of the following year, 1905, 'young David' was born at the Palace, for if Charles should die then David would inherit, and, after him his firstborn; unless the former's inheritance were shown to be illegal. Land meant a lot in those days, and David must have often regretted that he was rootless, a grave handicap among people whose handbook was *Burke's Landed Gentry*. If he or his son were to inherit that land-luck would be remedied. If it persisted, there was always his career to give him social standing; but if Charles were forced to abdicate in favour of the legitimate issue of their parents, that could be difficult to live with.

Ethel would have no such misgivings. So far as she knew David's inheritance, and now his son's, was assured; and Charles, though returned safely from the Boer War, lived dangerously. Just one bad fall when racing or hunting and she would be mistress of Borodale.

In contrast to these serious considerations of young David's future prospects, the happy throng which crammed the church at his christening behaved with such unbecoming levity that David was taken outside and reprimanded, by no less a person than the woman who ran the choir. 'I have spent three years trying to teach the boys to reverence the House of God and you bring your friends here and treat the church like the lounge of a theatre'. Unfortunately, David's retort, if any, went unrecorded. Not that it matters in comparison with this penetrating glimpse into the social climate of Malta at the period; more appropriate to a holiday resort than a naval base, at least from the point of view of sweethearts and wives. Naval Officers on duty were full of dark forebodings which they kept among themselves: the imminence of war. David held particularly unorthodox, and therefore unpopular, views. He and some like-minded officers did not conceal their anxiety lest the Royal Navy's antiquated technology and tactics should be found wanting when the the great test came. It was therefore another stroke of luck for David that he was sent back home before the displeasure of his seniors was officially expressed. The task before him was a daunting one: Naval Adviser to the Army Council. Specifically he was to plan the role of the Channel Fleet in protecting a British Expeditionary Force going over to France, and subsequently guaranteeing uninterrupted reinforcements, supplies, and equipment.

So, quite inadvertently, the authorities provided David with a forum not dominated by traditional thinking, least of all in naval matters. It must have been obvious to the Generals, if not to diehard Admirals, that the success of any such operation in support of a continental army, would depend upon British sea supremacy *before* the outbreak of war; and that, in turn, demanded immediate updating of the Fleets. Indeed, 1905 was another watershed year in that he then emerged from executive duties to cope with theory, policy and politics. In April he had been made a Member of the Victorian Order, and on the fifth of November became *Aide de Camp* to the King; but his ambition remained as always: active service.

Back to sea again, in his first battleship, *Queen*, he was shocked to discover that the only exercises permitted were still woefully out of date, taking no account of the high speeds, long ranges, and communications problems of war conditions as they were bound to be; still less of mines, submarines, torpedoes from destroyers against capital ships, and aircraft. Frustration mounted. He became a nuisance to the high command, and this would not be forgotten when, four years later, the Admiralty very nearly came to the conclusion that they had no more use for his services.

His tour of duty lasted for two years by which time he was again due for extended leave; so the summer of 1909 saw him with Ethel at Newmarket when Edward VII paid another of his not infrequent visits; since, following his coronation, the racing fraternity had presented him with a silver cup. The gift was handed to the King by Charles' head lad at Bedford Cottage, so it is not strange that, to the surprise of many, the shocked disapproval of a few, not only David but also Ethel was presented to His Majesty: an unheard of event since she had been divorced, and one which brought her the distinction of being the sole divorcée in the Royal Enclosure at Ascot that year, though the rule still held until as late as 1955.

As the year drew to its close his situation was doubly precarious. His career, – though he knew it not, was on the brink of disaster, not only because of impious ideas, officially expressed, but also because it was believed he really wanted to retire, being no longer dependent upon his pay. Yet he continued to follow his star though Ethel had again turned against him:—

'H.M.S. *Queen* Christmas 1909

I do hope, dear one, you are *happy*. It struck me very forcibly on my return that you did not seem so, and the afternoon we went down to Brooksby I felt as if I were an ogre dragging you to some fearful place you dreaded. You see, dear, your happiness is the one thing I live for, and if only you are happy and contented, so am I, but I fear I am making a hash of it somehow, and at times it appears that the point of a rift in the lute is inclined to show and I can't think why, but have a sort of intuition that it is there. God knows I do not wish at all times to force myself down your throat, but give me your confidence in all things. By plain speaking half the misery in the world could be done away with. A new year is about to begin. I shall arrive at a higher status in life at the same time with greater responsibilities and possibly greater opportunities, of which I shall want to make the most, and the first essential must be that I have you on my side, your advice, your assistance, and your confidence in all things. I have many faults. No one can see them more than you; won't you out of kindness point out where I fail, and in what I upset you, as it would appear I do at times? You have the instinct and could put your finger on the sore spot if you could only speak frankly and tell me wherein I fail, for I truly feel that I do fail, and I do so want to succeed in making you happy and not rub you up the wrong way. Will you try to understand me and this rigmarole?'

Somehow he weathered both storms. The jealous ones could find no rope with which to hang his reputation and, as usual, Ethel's aversion to him was short lived, in part because on the first day of 1910 he became Rear-Admiral and was appointed to a committee studying one of his pet projects, the foundation of a naval Staff College. True, he would not be commanding a ship, which in any other circumstances would have elicited a blistering protest, but if he had to be chair-borne, this was the best chair.

In this way David Beatty became one of the originators of a Staff training system originally sponsored by 'Jackie' Fisher when First Sea Lord, which would enable the Navy to become, from unit to flotilla, and squadron, to the integral of all units, the Grand Fleet, a projection from the mind of the appropriate Commander. Like fire-control, which used to be done by shouting, mind-control had never before demanded such extensions of the local responsibility of senior officers. Had the Portsmouth Staff College not been founded in time, the Germans might well, with their superior communications and a similar system of collective responsibility, have worn the British down to the point where defeat on land would have been inevitable. They nearly did – in spite of Jutland – when the submarine came into its own; and that was another future threat to which Beatty drew urgent attention, ahead of his time. For he was not a derring-doer rather than planner, nor was his idea of naval tactics anything like the 'cavalry spirit' which Churchill invoked in relation to the rôle of the battle cruisers. Not only did he think clearly; he saw, in addition to the submarine menace, other weapons still to come, visualising battles yet to be under conditions that never were.

After three months he left his comfortable chair and reasonably assumed that his efforts to update the antiquated system of training by tradition had been duly appreciated by their Lordships; but it was not so. Anyone with less self-assurance would have expected something of the sort, for, despite his Flag Rank, resistance to innovation was bound to persist, and with it went the view that to criticise his betters, or at least seniors, was close to insubordination. It is hardly surprising therefore that when he was again offered a sea appointment its standing was less than he had a right to expect: a snub. And when he declined the offer, as no doubt he felt obliged to, it was said that he did so out of arrogance and because, no longer being dependent on his pay, he really wanted to retire. Nothing could have been further from the truth. He was as keen on active service as ever, but, realising that once out of the main stream of policy-making he might never get back to it, he rightly took the risk of waiting for something better, and meanwhile continued to impress, upon anyone who would listen, that, as he said in a speech to the Lord Mayor at a Guildhall banquet, 'Never in the history of the world has there been such overwhelming preparation for war'. How could he help to prepare Britain if he were exercising a squadron in the Mediterranean?

Everything was subordinated to preparedness, even Ethel, and this she bitterly resented, perhaps more than on previous occasions because Society was now wide open to her, since Ascot; and nothing on her scale of values could be more important, for the word 'society' in those days referred only to 'those personally known to the Sovereign'. How unfair it was that David was working so hard she saw very little of him! For, at the back of her mind she very well knew that, despite her beauty, charm, and wealth, by herself she was still hardly better than a nobody.

What to do? The same as usual when she felt neglected. First came a storm of fury, then tears, followed by an orgy of self-pity. The brain-storm having subsided, there was only one course open to her: escape. So she flitted over to France, presumably alone, and would not communicate with him at all.

From Monte Carlo she moved eastward along the coast to Mentone, then Italy, looking for better luck in the casino there; but in this she was disappointed and, characteristically, responded by raising her stakes. They reached nearly a thousand pounds a go at modern rates, and, even among the big spenders, to lose fifteen thousand francs in eleven *jeux* would have been noteworthy. By now she must have had many acquaintances along the Coast, and a few friends, for she was ever a companionable person and felt as much at home in some grand hotel as in an English country house. A factor in this unusual taste was her income from the Marshall Field Trust, paid free of tax: rumoured to be worth some eighty thousand pounds a year. Such a sum is not mere money. It is power, and she used it freely in furtherance of her desires; sometimes regardless of the feelings of other people. Not that she worshipped money, or power, as such. Rather, she treated them as aids to her ambition, and when this clashed with David, who was above such petty matters, they necessarily fell apart and she often became ill out of frustration.

If such a diagnosis is even roughly correct, one can begin to understand why she sometimes behaved oddly to those whom she could not dominate; and why, having spent a fortune on international doctors, she gained no lasting benefit despite the absence of any identifiable disease. To be ill was her only escape from the cul-de-sac to which she had dragged her marriage, and the escape itself was only satisfying when it made others miserable, besides herself.

When she returned from abroad, to find David relegated to half pay, as on previous occasions she picked up the threads of her routine as though they had never been tangled; but, despite his lack of an official position, she still saw far too little of him for her comfort. Behind the scenes at the Admiralty he was still involved, often caught between the crossfire of feuding Lords, some of whom were irresponsible, abusive, and slanderous about each other; notably Fisher[1] and Beresford. These otherwise dignified figures, carrying great responsibilities, sometimes behaved like schoolboy bullies, as the following quotation from Richard Hough's *First Sea Lord* (Fisher) indicates:— It refers to the genesis of that persecution of Prince Louis of Battenburg, Marquis of Milford Haven and First Sea Lord, until Fisher virtually caused his resignation, in November 1914:—

'Lord Charles Beresford killed Louis by stages from the day he first acquired senior responsibility, from about 1907 on, thrusting his lance into his quarry with the pack of gutter journalists and cruel and bigoted "social" naval officers and their wives crying for blood behind him. Already in 1909 he was publicly calling him a German spy', (p. 336).

If malicious gossip, totally without foundation, did not spare even the King's cousin, head of the family which still lends its title to the royal House of Windsor-Mountbatten – under which name Princess Anne was married – imagination falters at what was being alleged against that upstart Irish sportsman David Beatty. It

[1] Admiral of the Fleet Lord Fisher of Kilverstone First Sea Lord 1904–1914.

is hardly less of a tribute to him than his capacity for leadership that he refused to be drawn into the disgraceful *melée*, just as he never published a line in his own defence. Even so, the allegations of 'side' i.e. conceit, 'interest' and, because of his wife's wealth, lack of dedication to the Service, did reach the Board of Admiralty where they very nearly brought his career to an abrupt and inglorious end.

Fisher could be as abusive as Beresford, accusing him of being 'time-serving and jealous', even, and this does seem incredible, of espionage. Beresford hit back, calling the First Sea Lord 'lunatic' or 'that Mulatto', a reference to his having been born in Ceylon. A more difficult situation for Beatty can hardly be conceived since Beresford – also known as 'a wild Irish sportsman' – had been his benefactor. And Fisher was his superior, without whose approval he had no future. So great was the stress that once again Ethel found herself, as she would see it, neglected. No matter how hard he tried to please her, or whether she made herself agreeable to him in order to please herself, between them a fissure opened in the common ground on which they stood: marriage. For it is clear by now that they were not, and never had been, complementary characters. Instead, they were opposites of the kind which exercise upon each other a compulsive attraction which in turn produces irrational aversion. The extraordinary thing is that, despite this, they managed to persuade nearly everyone except the immediate family that, Ethel's ill-health excepted, all was well with their relationship; though this was true only to the extent that for the most part they went on talking, writing, and reaching for each other across the chasm. Through thirty long years David never faltered in his loyalty to Ethel, surely the most subtle and most difficult of all his duties. Perhaps he shared with Charles a morality of which the latter thought so much that he had the following lines inscribed on a panel in the study at Bedford Cottage:—

> '*We pass through this world but once. If therefore there be any good thing that I may do, or any kindness I can show, let me not defer it nor neglect it, for I shall not pass this way again*'.

Not love exactly, but surely the next best thing, and without the hazards attending the former when unsupported by obligation and devotion. These qualities they both had, and if only Ethel could have appreciated how impossible it was for David to sustain the gathering momentum of his work and at the same time be at her beck and call, the gulf could have been bridged. Alas, she still expected him to spend his whole life in *her* service and consequently accused him of neglect. One curious result of this was that in order to give her the impression that she was not being left out of his great world, which she could never enter, he used to write with a minimum of discretion about matters which should have been highly confidential.

5
SIR DAVID 1910–1914

As usual, the rift between David and Ethel healed during her absence abroad and normal relations were re-established in the autumn of 1909. In the following April she gave birth to the second boy, Peter, at Brooksby Hall, their hunting-box near Leicester. Quite soon afterwards they took a short holiday together, leaving the baby in the care of Lu, who came by train from Newmarket, having married Charles in 1905. As I was born in October 1910 she must have been carrying me at the time, though perhaps was unaware of her condition. To go all that way was in any case a kind gesture for an apparently unimportant chore, but, had she excused herself, we might never have learned another important family secret which the Admiral had to bear, and put further strain on his already stressful marriage.

Almost from birth, Peter's eyes had been watery, and now the lids tended to stick together while he slept. At first, like everyone else, Lu did not imagine the condition could be anything serious, but when it became worse she used her position as Ethel's sister-in-law to call in the doctor. It then appeared that the baby was suffering from *Opthalmia Neonatarum*, a notifiable disease often passing unrecognised in the first few weeks, which can only be acquired from the mother during the process of birth or else from infected material, such as a towel. The latter is highly improbable in a household where cleanliness and nursing care were of the highest standards, so the probability is overwhelming that Ethel carried one or another of the several micro-organisms which can cause this distressing complaint and its dreaded complication, meningitis. While it is true that the common cause is *gonococcus*, it would be unjustifiable to assume that it was in this particular case.

There may have been another organism, which Ethel innocently and unwittingly harboured. See Appendix 'D'.

When David and Ethel returned, Lu hurried back to Newmarket to await my arrival in October and prepare for Christmas in Ireland; a routine journey, for the first time complicated because of Humpy, my Nanny, and me. Father used to carry a key for the door of our railway compartment so that he could prevent anyone else invading our privacy. The personnel also included Mother's maid, a manservant, and a couple of terriers.

Meanwhile, Peter was still being treated by frequent eye irrigations and the instillation of silver nitrate, the standard procedure; but it had not been possible to identify the pathogen, as would be done today. The local infection gradually cleared up, but, over a period of years it became evident that there were complications which support the hypothesis that the case was probably of venereal origin; though obviously there can be no certainty. All that here matters is that from the Spring of 1910 David and Ethel had to face the fact that she had somehow become infected and passed it on to Peter. The effect on her morbid temperament does not bear thinking about. It must have aggravated her malaise and been at least partly responsible for her decline.

It also affected David's character, though probably not for the worse. He was already strong enough to withstand mental anguish which would unhinge a lesser man; but the insult to his feelings was not only due to suspicions about Ethel's behaviour. There was nothing new about that. He must have known that he could not have been the boy's father. This was generally accepted in later years, and I, for one, was told, by his near relative, who the other man was. Even now it is only permissible to add that his was a well-known family of the British aristocracy. As Peter grew up Ethel made no secret of her embarrassment at his conspicuous disability when in company, and in private she often ignored, or even mocked him. Of this David certainly disapproved but did not interfere, even when the meningeal symptoms became so marked that, in addition to being almost blind, Peter could no longer control the nerve reflexes of his head and neck, making him slobber and appear uncouth. In contrast to Ethel's dislike and David's indifference his many friends admired and truly loved him.

We last met by chance, in Piccadilly after the war, when he told me he had been informed, that same day, by his oculist's assistant, that 'it is time somebody told you, you will be permanently blind'. Peter spoke without emotion of any kind. Perhaps he was numbed, because he had been led to believe that corneal grafts might save his sight. At one time he had to hang about in a Swiss hotel waiting for the doctors to telephone that they had a suitable donor, after an accident.

David must have known at least that I suspected Peter's paternity, and surmised that Lu would have told me about the opthalmia; which indeed she did. This, together with David's near certainty that, as heir to Borodale, I must know about the bastardy, accounts for the strangely ambivalent attitude he began to adopt towards me. Much of the time when we were together between the wars he was indeed avuncular in the sense of caring and guiding, but I was often aware of a different face behind the mask which he seldom took off. Did he imagine I might betray him? Hardly likely, since that would also betray my Father's memory, but suspicion is an irrational thing. Having for years harboured the nagging suspicion that somehow, through somebody, the truth would come out, was it not reasonable to regard me as the major risk?

On the larger scale it is clear that from 1910 he attained his full stature as a personality, and perhaps his ability to absorb these secrets into the texture of his character had something to do with it. No longer weakness to be feared, they served to toughen his already formidable armour. There would be no more children.

That he took no action, either against his wife or her lover, is hardly explicable save on such an assumption, but, knowing his temper, Ethel must have agonised lest she again find herself divorced. Peter the innocent had put in jeopardy all she had achieved since her second wedding, for if David instituted proceedings there would be no future for her in England, whatever the verdict of the Court. At thirty-six and with her record not even America would be likely to welcome her, and, although opthalmia had no legal bearing on the case, if it were mentioned at all it would be sure to win sympathy from the judge and headlines in newspapers on both sides of the Atlantic.

Whether David seriously considered such a step is a matter only for speculation. He must indeed have been deeply hurt, not least through one of the principal chinks in his armour: pride, but would shrewdly have recognised that publicity would be even more painful. And legal proceedings might well boomerang. Regardless of the rights of the case it might well damage, if not destroy, his career prospects, already far from bright; and without Ethel's income he would soon be relatively poor.

In January 1912 the issue of Beatty's future in the Navy at last crystallised in no uncertain terms. As Churchill recalls in *World Crisis*, 'Most of the Sea Lords were against giving him further employment', nor is the reason far to seek. He was thoroughly unpopular, if not out of jealousy then because of his demeanour, 'already developing into a caricature of his self-created image, his hair already far too long, his hat already at a sharp angle, his gestures over dramatic. But his powers of leadership had grown too and his courage had never been questioned.'[1]

'Most of the Sea Lords' must mean three out of four, so Fisher and Beresford voted against him, with Prince Louis of Battenberg as it were in the chair, at least concurring. It looks as though Beatty's efforts to accommodate the two inveterate enemies, to both of whom he was beholden, resulted, as so often happens, in them turning against him.

In the ordinary way such a verdict would have meant an immediate demand for his resignation, never again to feel the deck of a warship under his feet. That he not only survived but prospered in an entirely unlooked for direction was due to Winston Churchill's phenomenal memory. Now first Lord and therefore the political head of the Navy, he recalled what Steevens described as the 'gallant, disastrous and pointless charge of the 21st Lancers' at Omdurman. He also remembered a certain white gunboat in support of them, commanded by a David Beatty who, despite his very junior rank became during the campaign a personal friend of the Sirdar, Commander-in-Chief, Lord Kitchener of Khartoum. In those days 'K', as he was generally called, was regarded as an outstandingly good judge of men. If Beatty was good enough for him then, why, he must be good enough for the Government now, even with the whole Board of Admiralty against him.

[1] Hough (R): *The Battle of Jutland* (Hamish Hamilton 1964).

Never one to defer action, regardless of opposition, Churchill promptly cut through the red tape and evaded their Lordships' decision by appointing Beatty to his personal staff in the 'summit' post of Secretary to First Lord, which carried with it the unique privilege of intimate knowledge of naval matters world-wide and at the highest level. It suited David perfectly, and in that capacity he served with distinction from 8th January 1912 to February in the following year; by which time Churchill must already have decided that, far from being retired, he should in due course be invested with high command in the vast fleet gradually being organised.

It is unlikely that Churchill alone held this view for in the Spring of 1912 there came another lucky break for Beatty, aboard the Admiralty yacht *Enchantress*: of 4,000 tons, complete with boardroom, a cabin as big as the smoking room in a London club, very similarly furnished, and a magnificent 'cellar' of wine.

Despite serious business and forthright opinions it must have been a congenial voyage, ending with fleet manoeuvres employing the naval tactics evolved by the Portsmouth Staff College. Everything went according to plan except for a minor escapade for which Churchill was responsible: a secret meeting with the ageing Lord Fisher who had been First Sea Lord from 1904 to 1910, then resigned in dudgeon because he could not get his own way, and was now being courted with the idea that, even at seventy-one, he was the proper person to return to that high office under threat of war. More than anyone else he had been responsible for the dreadnaughts and battle cruisers. He had brought the fleet into being. Let him direct it when the fighting started, with his 'beloved' Jellicoe in executive command.

The reason for secrecy was principally Fisher's reputation for high-handed actions and irresponsible statements. The Press must on no account even suspect that the old man was about to be invited back to the Admiralty, and by his ex-enemy, Winston Churchill, of all people. So *Enchantress*, it was claimed, had to put in to Naples only because of bad weather; and that was where Fisher was staying as part of a regular sojourn abroad. He evidently knew nothing of the intention until he was invited aboard.

Burn   May 28th 1912
Secret and Private
My beloved Fiennes,[1]
     I was nearly kidnapped and carried off in the Admiralty yacht!
They were very sweet about it! My old cabin as First Sea Lord all
arranged for me! The Prime Minister is 'dead on' for my coming
back, and he has put things so forcibly to me that with great
reluctance to re-enter the battle field, I probably shall do so!

Indeed he did, only to resign again, in May 1915, amid many
protests not least from Jellicoe and Beatty; though it would soon
become clear that the maker of the modern navy was himself
obsolescent, like the ships which his dreadnaughts replaced, not
only in the Royal Navy, but world wide. *Enchantress* returned
home in the autumn, and at Portsmouth Beatty was told
confidentially by Churchill of the best offer that, as yet, he ever
had, the 'incomparable command' of the Battle Cruisers. This
decision had been arrived at, during the voyage, on the highest
political level, the Prime Minister in person, Asquith. In addition
to Churchill, there were Prince Louis and Lord Kitchener, with
their supporting staffs. So much for the censorious Sea Lords!
Instead of being 'on the beach' David Beatty had been chosen for
the unique distinction of leading the van of the Grand Fleet in the
Great War, now approaching.
     The appointment duly confirmed, he wrote:—

14 November 1912   Admiralty

Dear Mr Churchill,
                    It is with great pleasure I accept your offer of
the command of the First Battle Cruiser Squadron. It is indeed a
command to be proud of and I trust I shall justify your selection of
me by my administration of this very valuable and important unit.
                                   Yours sincerely,
                                        David Beatty

[1] Gerald Fiennes, naval journalist. It was not unusual at this period for
men as equals to use terms of endearment such as 'beloved'. See Hough
(R): First Sea Lord, p. 317.

He then left the Admiralty to set about working up his ships; no easy task, being of novel design in almost every particular. Hulls, engines, guns, rangefinders and communications were all difficult to 'shake down' with a crew of at least a thousand men, few of whom had been in such a vessel before. Even so, in less than five months the squadron was up to the mark, and David, after such an arduous and anxious time, between the decision to retire him and this 'incomparable command', set out blithely for Monte Carlo. There he joined Ethel, in March 1913, taking with him the best of all possible gifts, a wonderful and exciting mission in which she could fully share: no less than a diplomatic voyage with the aim of persuading the Russians to become our allies against Germany. All gloom forgotten, for the first time they would be on duty together. He would not have to remind her that his position was now such that never again must there be the slightest pretext for anyone to suspect that the marriage had been unstable, and could collapse under stress. Human nature does not change, nor do mature personalities. The instability was always there, yet they remained together, which was no mean achievement.

That his dedication to work still allowed him to play is indicated by an illuminating incident with which he must have regaled Ethel as being a great joke. As such it became part of the Beatty legend though perhaps not so greatly to his credit as at first appears.

In March 1913 his Squadron was anchored off Weymouth, but he was relaxing in London, expected to rejoin *Lion* from a train due in at about midnight. He was too late to catch the train, and around eleven o'clock hailed a taxi in Piccadilly, telling the driver to make for Weymouth in a hurry; for the squadron had his own orders to sail at dawn. The distance by modern roads is over a hundred and thirty miles. According to Lieutnant R. Schwerdt, who had the Middle Watch in *Lion* that night, the Admiral was brought aboard his barge at about three in the morning, apologising because the driver had twice lost his way. The superficial aspect of the journey as some kind of lark does nothing to mask its serious implication: that instead of telegraphing to the station master at Weymouth to tell the crew of the barge to warn the flagship of the Admiral's delayed arrival he elected to take what in those days was a really hazardous journey; in a taxi of primitive performance not at all designed for grand touring.

It must have been cold. Roads were poor. Signposts, when they could be picked out in the light from acetylene headlamps, confusing indeed for a London cabby, who had probably never been farther than Margate. Yet he managed to average a shade over thirty miles an hour! Meanwhile, the Captain of *Lion* had sensibly gone to bed, leaving his Lieutenant to sort out any tangles, and to report the squadron ready for sea at dawn. The barge's crew had no alternative but to wait until the Admiral appeared, and the midshipman in command must have been somewhat embarrassed when he emerged from the taxi. Beatty's last remark before going below was, 'Let the barge's crew have a lie-in. I'm sorry I'm late.'

It was not like him to be plain stupid, yet that is how the escapade appears by hindsight; nor inconsiderate. And failure to warn Weymouth can hardly be judged otherwise.

Despite the British entente with Japan, traditional enemy of Russia, Admiralty planning had long been directed towards a Russian alliance, and in pursuit of this aim the Government had solicited an invitation for the battle cruisers to visit the naval base of Kronstadt at the mouth of the river Neva in the gulf of Finland. This would involve a voyage of over a thousand miles, across the North Sea, round the tip of Denmark, through the length of the Baltic, a route not without navigational hazards for warships bigger than any which had previously entered those waters. On the last leg they would call at Reval, now Tallin, where in 1904 Edward VII paved the way for this rapprochement by making such a good impression that Germany became suspicious that an alliance might, even then, be directed against her. Ten years later German anxiety on that score was well founded, particularly a fear that in the event of war the Royal Navy would dominate the Baltic with the intention of securing safe passage for Russian troops to invade the Fatherland. This plan was in fact proposed by Fisher, only to be overruled by Churchill in favour of the Dardanelles adventure of 1915. The quarrel between them never healed and Fisher resigned, for the second time, in May of that year.

The earliest acceptable date for the visit was May 1914, and this was welcomed by the Admiralty. No detail, however small, escaped their attention, and, with their vast resources it seemed there was nothing they could not do to make this delicate mission a diplomatic coup under cover of a mere social occasion, – except provide a hostess for the hospitality the Squadron would have to give, both afloat and ashore. Since the Admiral would have his hands full without that additional burden, it was agreed that his wife should be at hand for the purpose, assisted by Lady Gwendolin Churchill.

Because of exigencies of the Service, and also the bare possibility that Germany might anticipate a British presence in the Baltic by launching a surprise attack, without declaration of war, Ethel could not take passage in *Lion*; so arrangements were made for her yacht to sail independently and moor to a buoy conveniently placed in Kronstadt harbour. This opened up a daunting prospect for her, not only because she would, for most of the time, be separated from David, but also in view of the constant surveillance by Cheka, as the Secret Police were then known. If anyone could pin the slightest irregularity on the steam yacht *Sheelah* or any of her complement the success of the mission might be jeopadised.

So, in this theatrical manner, an American whose father was 'in trade' and therefore below the salt according to Russian protocol, was presented at the stuffiest Court in Europe, more or less On His Majesty's Service. And if that seems absurd one only needs to remember that through his friendship with George V, David, and therefore Ethel, were indeed acceptable to his cousin Nicholas II, Tsar of all the Russias.

On the morning of 20th June, the squadron, consisting of *Lion*, *Queen Mary*, *Princess Royal* and *New Zealand*, entered harbour with ponderous dignity and meticulous drill. They drew so much water that a channel had been specially dredged for them and furnished with buoys with particularly heavy anchors. The weather was perfect and crowds of people lined the shore, most of whom had come down the forty kilometres from St Petersburg by ferry on the river Neva; though there were also rail and road connections. On board, preparations went ahead for arduous entertainment:—

'We found our ten days at Kronstadt an almost intolerable strain, but they certainly did not lack in interest or excitement. St Petersburg life started at 11 p.m.; the day was hot and the daylight extended practically through the night. We had an enormous mass of hospitable invitations; invitations to the Admiral and officers with this and that municipality, to seamen to attend banquets and theatres in St Petersburg. And, as Chief of Staff, I had to arrange everything. The difficulty was to make our ship life suit Russian hours. Officers and men did not return on board until 5 a.m.; every ship had to play her part and provide the required numbers for the innumerable functions; hospitality nearly ran us off our legs.'[1]

For the Admiral and his Captains the first, and most important function was to present themselves formally to the Tsar. This involved much protocol and almost oriental splendour, from the gilded carriages which conveyed them to Tsarskoe Selo, a group of palaces unchanged since the time of Catherine the Great, through luncheon presided over by the Tsarina and four Grand Duchesses, to an appreciation of at least part of this extraordinary estate, with its seven hundred acres of lawns, its gorgeous officials, and a round-the-clock patrol of Cossacks. The Admiral was much put out on returning to Kronstadt to find he was expected to tip each of the coachmen.

On the following day the courtesy was returned and the Imperial Family, with four teenage daughters and the Grand Duchesses, were shown round *Lion*, then given a luncheon on board (at which Ethel was present) nor was that the end of this red-letter day. Far from it. Two thousand guests were to attend a dinner in *Lion* and dance all night on *New Zealand*, laid alongside and bridged together. Both ships were dressed overall, with searchlights fore and aft to play on the flags, particularly the Imperial Standard and the White Ensigns. Though he did not hear of it till later, on this day the Admiral received his knighthood in the third senior Order after the Garter and the Thistle, becoming a Knight Commander of the Most Honourable Order of the Bath, so called because in medieval times the candidate was given a ritual bath before his all night vigil in the chapel.

Dinner that night was served in the Russian manner, consisting of two separate stages, in different places. First came a luxuriant display of elaborate cold dishes, hors d'oeuvres, caviar, and of course, champagne and vodka. Then, on deck the formal meal, at

---

[1] Chatfield (Lord): *The Navy and Defence.*

two hundred circular tables, each seating six, which had been run up by the ships' carpenters from rum casks and planking. That so many could have been accommodated gives an indication of the great beam of these vessels which conveyed to all who saw them a sense of overwhelming power, – as was intended. Sir David personified that power:—

' . . . the youngest British Admiral since Nelson made a tremendous impression. His youthful, clean-shaven face caused many Russians, accustomed to seeing admirals with beards to their waists, to mistake Beatty for his own Flag Lieutenant. But Beatty's manner was unmistakably one of command. His square jaw and the jaunty angle at which he wore his cap suggested the sea dog. He spoke in a voice which would have carried over the howl of a gale. It was as if the solid reality of Britain's enormous seapower, a thing few Russians understood, had suddenly become revealed in Beatty's person.'[1]

The material basis of his authority was equally impressive, for the Battle Cruiser Squadron, though only a fraction of the Grand Fleet and an even smaller factor in Britain's world-wide naval presence, was without precedent. Bald figures give only an intimation of what it meant at Kronstadt in that last June before the whirlwind struck. In company with her sister ships, *Lion* carried eight 13·5 inch guns, with fifteen 4 inch as secondary armament and two submerged torpedo tubes. She displaced 26,350 tons, was capable of 28 knots, and had a fuel capacity of 4,600 tons of coal.

Upon the 'reception area' of this monstrous fortress, Ethel Beatty received her distinguished guests, that is to say under an awning over the quarterdeck, now garlanded with coloured lights, bunting and flowers. Because Royalty had honoured the Admiral by their presence at luncheon the four Grand Duchesses were the guests pre-eminent, followed by everybody who was anybody in the Capital. The scale of the all night party was such that, in addition to supplies brought out from home, the Admiral commandeered the Embassy's stock of champagne, one thousand two hundred bottles.

To have been presented to the Tsar must have rejoiced Ethel.

---

[1] From an eyewitness quoted in *Nicholas and Alexandra* by R. K. Massie (Gollancz 1968).

Not many women could claim that they may have helped to change the course of history by entertaining the last absolute monarch in the western world.

Particularly for the Admiral, Russian hospitality was not without hazards. Many years later he told me how at a formal dinner given by senior Russian officers, he realised that it was their intention to make him drunk: a usual Russian ploy. Naturally I sympathised with him, torn apart between giving offence by refusing toasts and the grave risk of becoming indiscreet, if not incapable. 'How on earth did you cope?' I asked.

The deadpan answer was, 'Drank them under the table and walked back to my ship.' Not that he could have walked all the way, for *Lion* was still at her buoy.

Standart was the largest of the Imperial Yachts, and equipped to be a floating palace. There were crystal chandeliers, parquet floors, and a series of reception rooms, all within a hull big enough for a light cruiser; which also housed a detachment of Marines. After the jollity afloat and ashore it may have been something of an anticlimax when she followed the Squadron to sea at its departure. Then the Admiral made his final gesture in pursuance of the diplomatic object of the visit. While the Tsar watched from the bridge of his enormous yacht the battle cruisers performed complicated evolutions at twenty-five knots, demonstrating that behind their colossal fire-power lay a capacity for manoeuvre and high speed which gave them, at least in theory, a lead over every other class of warship.

Whether Russian entry into the war was in fact influenced by the impression gained by the Tsar of an apparently invincible Britannia, despite his extensive knowledge of the German High Seas Fleet, is still arguable; but it must have counted for something. Also there was the personal equation, perhaps equally important, and that included Ethel.

Despite the luxurious vulgarity of the Kronstadt parties, they are today more memorable as symptoms of decadence at the end of an era. Within three months, all concerned would be hitched to a chain of events which led to the disintegration of the Old Order in Europe and would drag the Tsar, his body politic, his family and himself to ignominious and cruel destruction. Out of this bloodbath a New Order would arise, to institute an even greater tyranny. . . . It was scientifically assured that a dynastic quarrel would lead to the death, not of thousands but of millions of men. In the upheaval of such murderous wars lay the promise of revolution. 'A war with Austria would be a splendid thing for the Revolution' Lenin wrote to Maxim Gorky in 1913, 'but the chances are small that Franz Josef and Nicholasha will give us such a treat.'[1]

With all its faults the Old Order had principles, even virtues, which today are in short supply because they were rooted in the soil of patriotism, conceived as an ideal of service which transcended material considerations.

Not believing for a moment that the British Empire would ever disintegrate, Kipling wrote its epitaph with the reiterated warning, 'Lest we forget.' Forget what? Not only those who needlessly died, in battle some twelve million between 1914 and 1918, but also that they did so because most of them really believed in idealism. The Old Order would never deny spirit, for by it were they ensouled. Today most people are very willing to forget the values of yesterday, and in their forgetting are entrapped by drab materialism, which knows the price of everything and the value of nothing. Of the few who do remember our decline and fall, the older generation, they too prefer not to be reminded how Kipling's doom did come to pass:—

> Far-called our navies melt away –
> On dune and headland sinks the fire –
> Lo, all our pomp of yesterday
> Is one with Nineveh and Tyre!

In terms of force as material power certainly our fires are sinking, but spirit is more than power and, at the same time, its origin. Only the outward forms change. So long as the ashes glow the immaterial essence is still there, of life perpetually renewed. It happened in 1939 when a generation generally regarded as effete instinctively embodied 'our pride of yesterday'. The nearest thing to the Battle of Jutland was the Battle of Britain. The Dolphin of Admiralty had grown Phoenix wings, and unless we again forget

[1] Massie (R. K.) op. cit.

to tend its fire, yet another generation may be kindled from it, to fight perhaps in machines as yet unknown; but to the same high purpose.

In that light the obvious standard by which to assess the naval effort in the first World War is in terms of material, the outward sign and consequence of the inward cause. Of the Spithead Review 1914 Churchill wrote, 'It constituted incomparably the greatest assemblage of naval power ever witnessed in the history of the World.' Another eyewitness,[1] uses similar language, 'The greatest navy which had ever existed. The impact upon all who witnessed it was enough to last a lifetime.' Yet what they saw, – some thirty miles of warships in seven columns – was but one element of world-wide supremacy; and within four years that element would increase more than sixfold. Let the full muster speak for itself.

Total of warships and others under
Admiralty control:

	1914	1918
Warships	648	1,354
Auxiliaries	12	3,727
	660	5,081

If to those figures are added the losses sustained during the war, and they were considerable, this means that the Navy's strength at the end of the struggle was of the order of ten times what it had been at the beginning. The comparison does more than demonstrate what naval supremacy then meant. It shows why the Royal Navy, aided by the Americans, from 1917 onwards, constituted the overriding factor, political and economic as well as offensive, which made Allied victory inevitable.

Soon after the Peace, however, scrapyards were busier than shipyards . . . 'I counted them at break of day, and in the evening where were they?' Though only a few, and Beatty was among

[1] Massie (R. K.) op.cit.

them, foresaw the future role of aircraft, many would soon have reason to be thankful that the spirit which fought the fleets entered the Royal Air Force. Far-fetched? Strange things happen in the depths of the collective mind to give a nation the ability continually to adapt. Our Admiral was more than vaguely aware of something of the sort, and if that is what people sometimes refer to as his 'superstition' we may accept it as something more than such quaint concessions to the lore as bowing to the New Moon or affirming that the souls of drowned sailors 'take up their abode in wild sea birds.' He really believed in the guiding hand of Destiny, otherwise *le bon Dieu*, and in his lifetime foresaw, as did few others, the great air fleets of the morrow. Had he been able to witness the Battle of Britain, or that airborne armada of 1944–1945 which, again aided from across the Atlantic, pulverised Germany's heartland, he would surely have recognised in those aircrews the heirs of his own ships' complements. For those in whom it dwells the spirit is one and indivisible. It is also permanent as a law of nature, and ensouls whatever vehicles, human or otherwise, are appropriate to its operations at a particular place and time.

Returned from Russia, justified in his command, at one with Ethel, and, above all, confident in those superb ships; on leave David found all things well. Brother Charles had moved from Newmarket to Atherstone, leaving the business of training winners to the younger brother, Vandy. Charles became joint Master of the Atherstone hounds and, outside the hunting season, built a Stud Farm at Borodale, from which promising thoroughbreds would go to Vandy for training. It was a workable and efficient partnership which promised better financial reward than farming could provide. Why so many commitments when he knew, like David, that war was imminent? The answer must be, that, like most well-informed people, both now expected a quick contest. A weekly publication stored at Borodale, *The Army and Navy Gazette* in an issue at the beginning of August 1914, contained a serious Editorial to the effect that though Officers were bound to miss the grouse shooting, they would surely be back in time for December pheasants, having disposed of the German horde.

If to hindsight this seems both stupid and arrogant, one must remember that the last fleet action had been at Trafalgar in 1805: a few hours cannonade which secured naval peace for a century. The last campaign in the field had been against the Boers, which, according to Whitehall's thinking at the time, only dragged on for two years because the enemy knew their own country better than did the invaders. No one in England, or indeed Europe, could have been expecting a long war, either naval or military. The Germans planned for a grand offensive, the Schlieffen plan, which would put their armies on the Channel coast in weeks. Accordingly they had no need to risk a fleet action, though obstinately and against all the evidence, the Admiralty did. The principle they worked on was that the capital ship is the sovereign of the seas. Therefore the enemy must seek to destroy, if not the battle fleet, at least detached portions of it; and the sooner the better because otherwise their mercantile shipping would be swept from the oceans of the world: as indeed it was.

As for land battles, how could two cavalry-minded armies have envisaged something which had never happened before in the entire history of warfare: trenches and barbed wire? Add that both Services firmly believed that modern fire-power, never put to the test except on exercises, must make prolonged conflict impossible, so great would be the immediate destruction.

It was into this foggy climate of thought and with dire forebodings that David and Charlie went their separate ways, when, having been together nearly all their lives, they parted in July 1914, David went to the Fleet for the Spithead Review and thence, on mobilisation, into the grey North. They would meet again only once, at Charlie's bedside in 1916. Unfit for service owing to wounds received in the South African war, Vandy was left to carry on business at Newmarket. Lu had to go over to Ireland to see how the management of the estate could be carried on until the return of 'the Major'.

On mobilisation, the Commander-in-Chief Grand Fleet, – which used to be called the Channel Fleet – was Sir George Callaghan, who should have retired the previous year but had been requested to stay on. To him Sir David Beatty was directly responsible, though the Battle Cruiser Force had a degree of autonomy when actually at sea. Sir John Jellicoe was at the Admiralty as Second

Sea Lord, and expected to remain there. Then, on the 30th July he learned, from First Lord and First Sea Lord, that there might be a change of command 'in certain circumstances'. He was to journey north immediately, report to the Commander-in-Chief at Scapa Flow and there await developments. He left London the same day, and during the long trip by rail and boat had plenty of time to form his own impression of what might be afoot. This led to the conclusion that the best place for him would be as Callaghan's assistant or Chief of Staff.

Arrived at the anchorage, he duly reported, without saying anything of what was in his mind. Instead, the two admirals discussed what ship would be most suitable for Jellicoe's flag.

'About 4 a.m. on August 4th,' he wrote in his book, *The Grand Fleet*, 'I received Admiralty orders to open a secret envelope which had been handed to me in the train as I was leaving London, by an officer from the Admiralty.'

The letter reads as follows:—

July 31st 1914   Admiralty

I am commanded by the Lords Commissioners of the Admiralty to inform you that, in the circumstances that will have arisen when the present letter will have been opened, they have been pleased to select you to be Commander-in-Chief of the Grand Fleet in succession to Admiral Sir George Callaghan. You are, therefore, on receipt of orders to open this letter, to repair with it on board H.M.S. *Iron Duke*. Show it to Sir George Callaghan as your authority for so doing and arrange with him for whatever immediate steps may be necessary to make your succession to the command effective. Thereafter Sir George Callaghan will come on shore.

(signed) W. Graham Greene
Permanent Secretary to the Admiralty

The crisp official sentences give no hint of the heart-searching this drastic action caused, not only to the retiring Admiral and his successor but also to Beatty, who added his protest to Jellicoe's. They were shocked and dismayed by the order, however expedient it might be in the corridors of power; because Callaghan was an old friend, a trusted comrade, who deserved a better fate than to be dismissed on the very threshold of the conflict for which most of his life had been spent in training; and with no notice at all. Jellicoe continues:—

'It was decided that I should take over command on the following day but a telegram having been received from the Admiralty ordering the Fleet to proceed to sea at once, I returned to the *Iron Duke* and Sir George Callaghan arranged to leave the Fleet in the *Sappho* before its departure at 8.30 next morning.

At that hour I took over command from Sir George Callaghan, who then struck his flag.'

Also at 8.30 a.m. on the first day of the war. . . .

'The Grand Fleet proceeded to sea in accordance with Admiralty orders. The vessels accompanying the fleet flagship *Iron Duke* were the vessels of the 1st, 2nd, 3rd and 4th Battle Squadrons, the light cruisers *Southampton*, *Birmingham*, *Boadicea*, *Blonde* and the destroyers of the 4th Flotilla; the cruisers *Shannon*, *Natal*, *Roxburgh* and the light cruisers *Nottingham*, *Falmouth and Liverpool* . . .'

At the same hour the Battle Cruiser Force proceeded to sea:—
'1st Battle Cruiser Squadron:

Vice-Admiral (acting) Sir David Beatty, K.C.B. (in command) Battleships *Lion* (Flag), *Princess Royal, Queen Mary, New Zealand*.'
It is notable that Sir John Jellicoe refers to these vessels as battleships, presumably because of their capability being equal to that of 'true' battleships with bigger guns but lower speed. Sir David was accompanied on that first 'sweep' of the North Sea by the 1st, 2nd, and 3rd Cruiser Squadrons, of four ships each, and 2nd, 4th Destroyer Flotillas; in all 56 ships. Such was the Battle Cruiser Force at the very start of the great conflict, semi-independent of the Commander-in-Chief yet forming part of the Grand Fleet under his orders.

The nature of these in turn stemmed from Admiralty policy:—
'The orders under which the Fleet acted were to sweep east as far as long 2 E and then for the cruisers to carry out a wide sweep to the southward and south-westward. These orders were in conformity with the general strategical ideas embodied in the War Orders for the Grand Fleet, which aimed at establishing a Blockade; and preventing enemy forces from getting into the

Atlantic to interfere with the operations of our cruisers engaged in protecting our own trade as well as stopping trade on behalf of the enemy; and at asserting control of the North Sea and denying it to the enemy. Pursuant to these orders, the 1st Battle Cruiser Squadron and the 3rd Cruisers squadron were directed to sweep . . .'

At midnight the Admiralty signalled, 'Commence hostilities against Germany' and the King sent the following message by wireless telegraphy to his Commander-in-Chief:—

'At this grave moment in our National history, I send to you, and through you to the officers and men of the Fleet of which you have assumed command, the assurance of my confidence that under your direction they will revive and renew the old glories of the Royal Navy, and prove once again the sure Shield of Britain and of her Empire in the hour of trial.'

While all this was going on, thousands upon thousands of men were streaming through recruiting offices into training camps where reservist officers and other ranks were already established. On the eleventh of August, by which time the fleet had returned to Scapa, the Acting Vice-Admiral's brother, Charles, 'The Major', received the following telegram at Borodale, redirected from Atherstone:—

'Major Beatty, Borodale Enniscorthy

Would you like to come as *aide de camp* to me mounted force home defence at first.

Alderson, Angel Hotel, Bury St Edmunds.'

The reply was a foregone conclusion, for Charles had been the General's *aide de camp* throughout the South African War, during which he won the D.S.O. and a row of campaign medals. So it is hardly surprising that he quickly set his affairs in order, if he had not done so already, and by 12th September, wrote his first letter to me, aged almost four:—

> Headquarters First Mounted Division
> Bury St Edmunds

'My dear Little Puppy Dog,
I got your very nice letter safely telling me all the news and how

you have been working so hard on the Farm and all about the Terrier.

Mummy and Nanny both say you have been such a good Boy and I hope you are taking good care of Mummy and don't let her work too hard.

There are such a lot of soldiers here, with great big guns to shoot the Germans with, and on Sunday bands play and they all go to church.

Goodbye, dear little Sonny, and take good care of your Mummy.

With much love from
Your old Daddy

Give Mummy a hug and a kiss from me.'

He would soon be in France, and when he returned, wounded, to England, it would be on borrowed time; for he died as the result of his injuries, in May 1917.

Though in itself of course the quoted letter is of no importance, yet it constitutes a pathetic indication of the heart-wrenching that was going on in the first few months of the war.

6

ACTION STATIONS
(1914–1916)

POST OFFICE   OFFICE OF ORIGIN
TELEGRAPHS   Edinburgh handed in 11.35 a.m.
OFFICE STAMP
Bury St Edmunds 29th August 1914 received 12.39 p.m.

TO Major Beatey Head Quarters Mounted Division Bury St Ed
    Splendid news from First Battle Cruiser Squadron
    no damage to ships or men
                            Ethel Beatey

(Now very frail but clearly legible, the original telegram is
scrawled in soft pencil.)

The engagement referred to became known as the Battle of the
(Heligoland) Bight, first heavy-ship action since the Japanese
eliminated the Russians at Tsushima in 1904, and the first occasion
on which battle cruisers fired main armament in anger, –
though not against vessels of their own class. In the main, this
close encounter was between light forces. Even so it became
another factor in the irrational belief that the High Seas Fleet
would soon challenge the Grand Fleet to a contest the like of
which was never before seen. Our Admiral's part in the action
was brief.

'Between 12.37 p.m. and 1.45 p.m.' wrote Jellicoe, 'the 1st
Battle Cruiser Squadron and the 1st Light Cruiser Squadron
engaged two other German light cruisers, one of which was sunk,

the second was last seen burning furiously and in a sinking condition.'

So Ethel's information was correct. A question remains as to how she received, and why she passed on, such intelligence; yet this she continued to do, particularly to Lu, her sister-in-law, so the quoted wire may be taken as typical of many. Whatever the means by which she gained such information, it was efficient. To quote Jellicoe again, 'The 1st Battle Cruiser Squadron (Beatty) arrived at Scapa to fuel at 7 p.m.' That refers to the 29th, but Ethel sent her telegram eight hours earlier, so either she must have been shown a signal – highly improbable – or someone telephoned. Because she happened to be in Edinburgh, this is unlikely, which makes the security angle even more acute, since it is hardly credible that any responsible Officer would have authorised the relay of a signal other than through approved channels and to an authorised recipient. All letters from the Fleet were censored. Even when C-in-C our Admiral had to frank, with initials, the stamped black circle on an envelope.

It is also of interest that, while Ethel is right about there being no damage to the Squadron, a light cruiser in the same action suffered 'considerable damage and several casualties'.

'The light cruiser *Mainz* had been attacking the somewhat disabled *Arethusa* and the *Fearless* at about 11.30 a.m. (27th August) and had suffered very severely in the action, being practically disabled[1]. . . .'

Ethel's telegrams imply no more than the casual attitude of the public to what we now call Security, yet it is still extraordinary that she should have addressed a senior Staff Officer at his Divisional Headquarters. Allowing that legitimately, and with nothing but good intent, she passed on what she learned owing to her privileged position, it should have occurred to her that Army Intelligence might think such communications peculiar, to say the least; since they came from a former American citizen many of whose countrymen were by no means committed to the Allied cause at this date.

As to why she was in Edinburgh, – she was looking for a house to which David could call home when he came ashore. Here too she seems to have inside information, for the word went round

[1] Jellicoe *ibid*.

that she had 'asked the Battle Cruisers to be sent to her address.' Absurd of course, but, while 'everyone' knew that the Grand Fleet lay at Scapa, a plan to detach Beatty's command and base it on Rosyth in the Firth of Forth, much further south, was very secret; because, if the enemy knew, he might profit from the division of our forces, gaining considerable advantage thereby if he could overwhelm the Battle Cruisers with his own Battle Fleet, or part of it, before Jellicoe could bring effective support from Scapa.

As usual, Ethel found what she wanted, Aberdour House, only seven miles from the dockyard, where for some years she lived almost alone except for Peter, aged five, and local social contacts, including naval wives in a similar but less opulent case. It is not surprising that her alternating moods of depression and euphoria returned, giving her the reputation of being somewhat 'mental', and incurring displeasure from dour Scots because of her occasionally lavish hospitality while her husband was virtually confined to his ship.

Then she made a gesture which disarmed some of the gossips. Having brought her yacht to the Firth of Forth she offered it to the Admiralty as a hospital ship. The offer was accepted and she then engaged one of the foremost surgeons of the day, Sir Alfred Fripp, to design the medical layout, particularly an operating theatre. This he did, and his ideas were subsequently incorporated in other hospital ships of more impressive tonnage. In this she found a worthwhile, even compelling interest, and it would be unkind not to concede that were she the best balanced woman in the world, as months became years up there, the strain must have been enough to crack almost anyone.

At sea nothing warlike happened – apart from submarines and mines – to break the dreary yet perilous routine. Even at anchor no ship was ever safe, and more than one blew up by spontaneous combustion of unstable explosive (Lyddite). Meanwhile, the armies were digging the foundations of the biggest shambles in history, and already in almost every British village there was a mourning of widows and the mothers of lost sons. Churchill, now at the Ministry of Munitions, condensed this monstrous inhumanity into a single sentence, 'We were the bees of hell, and we stored our hives with the pure essence of slaughter.'[1]

---

[1] *World Crisis II*, p. 482.

The greatest concentration of that essence was hived in the long grey ships, as would be tragically demonstrated when, seeming impregnable, their great guns blazing through their smoke, battle cruiser after battle cruiser disintegrated in seconds, sank in a few minutes. In the autumn of 1914 Jellicoe faced one of his most difficult tasks short of fleet action. Between the third and eleventh of October the First Division of the Canadian Expeditionary Force crossed the Atlantic for France, and to protect the transports a major portion of the Grand Fleet was detached on convoy duty in the area of greatest risk, between the Shetlands and Norway. Ahead of them, far into the Atlantic, the battle cruisers made rendezvous with the troop-carriers; so the men beside whom Charles Beatty would fight were met in mid-ocean by his brother David. It is a measure of Jellicoe's administrative competence that, just as with the conveyance and supply of the British Army across the Channel, there were no casualties or damage among the Canadians.

That winter, in weather seldom less than foul, the Fleet continued those frustrating sweeps, interspersed with gunnery exercises and perpetual chores, one of the worst of which was coaling. No stocks were carried ashore, so huge quantities had to be manhandled from colliers lying alongside in the seaway. Oil-firing had been introduced, thanks to Fisher, as early as 1912, but the adaption of stokeholds and boiler-rooms was a slow business and since oil had to be imported while coal was readily available in unlimited quantity, oil was not given the priority which some thought it deserved. There were certainly two arguments against fuel oil. In the first, that critical factor in battle, maximum knots, would not be improved by changing over. In the second there was so much desperately urgent work to be done, as for instance in sea defences against submarines and improvements of dockyards that the coal/oil issue was almost academic. A third factor was also taken into account. It was known that coal bunkers effectively cushioned underwater impact, as from armour-piercing shell, but no one knew what effect it would have on oil bunkers and many feared they would explode, or at least ignite.

Gales and rain added to the discomfort of living afloat. *Lion* leaked – even in the Admiral's cabin. With the coming of snow and ice, getting ships in and out of harbour became almost as hazardous as making contact with the enemy. One dark night in dense fog two destoyers went ashore against a cliff, and of their complements only four men managed to climb to safety from the sea. Of these, two froze to death before a rescue party could reach them next morning. Morale was still maintained, but how long could it last in such conditions?

Meanwhile, on land the stale-mate seemed complete, so when the next naval action took place, at Dogger Bank, on the 4th January 1915, it did wonders for the spirits of the whole country, including the army, as well as for the fleet although it was in fact but a modest, small-scale victory, offset by such severe damage to *Lion* that she had great difficulty in returning to Rosyth, even on tow.

She had been struck below the water-line by two heavy shells which pierced a boiler feed-tank, displaced an armour plate, and consequently flooded the port engine room. There were only eleven casualties, none fatal, a surprisingly light tally which increased confidence in the ability of the ships to take punishment; later proved to be misplaced. The only other battle cruiser to be damaged was *Tiger*, with five killed and eleven wounded. Action opened at 9.35 a.m. and 17,000 yards, with five British against four German battle cruisers. Of these, one (*Blücher*) sank and two (*Derflinger* and *Seydlitz*) were severely damaged. There were no survivors from *Blücher* because a Zeppelin tried to bomb rescue boats, and she would have had a complement of about a thousand. The other two vessels between them lost about 400, killed or wounded. Here is part of Beatty's official despatch:—

'At 11.20 a.m. I called the *Attack* alongside,[1] shifting my flag to her about 11.35 a.m. I proceeded at utmost speed to rejoin the Squadron, and met them at noon retiring N.N.W.

I boarded and hoisted my flag in *Princess Royal* at about 12.20 p.m. when Captain Brock, acquainted me with what had occurred since the *Lion* fell out of the line, namely that the *Blücher* had been sunk and the enemy battle Cruisers had continued their course to the eastward in a considerably damaged condition. . . .

At 2 p.m. I closed *Lion* and received a report that her starboard engine was giving trouble owing to priming, and at 3.38 I ordered

---

[1] *Attack* was a destroyer (Lieutenant Commander James).

Indomitable to take her in tow, which was accomplished at 5 p.m.

The greatest credit is due to the Captains of *Indomitable* and *Lion* for the seamanlike manner in which the *Lion* was taken in tow under difficult circumstances. . . .

Where all did well it is difficult to single out Officers and Men for special mention, and as *Lion* and *Tiger* were the only ships hit by the enemy, the majority of these I mentioned belong to those ships.

I have the honour to be, Sir,

Your obedient Servant

(signed) David Beatty

Vice-Admiral

That Beatty's leadership was based as much on his capacity for inspiring loyalty, even under the most arduous conditions, as upon professional skill, is emphasised by most writers, but, for obvious reasons, it is today difficult to come by heartwarming witness to it. The following letter is from Lieutenant E. G. Wye, R.N. retired, and is dated 16th June 1979:—

Dear Mr Beatty,

I served in *Princess Royal* under command of your uncle Sir David Beatty from 1913 until he became Commander-in-Chief of Grand Fleet and think the following incident well shows the high regard and esteem we lower deck ratings felt for him.

It was at the Battle of Dogger Bank. I was on the sick list, with both my hands badly frost bitten at Halifax Nova Scotia on our way back to rejoin the 1st Battle Cruiser Squadron, so had no action station.

When the firing ceased and we seemed to reduce speed, I went to the after 4″ gun deck and saw the *Lion* dropping astern with a slight list and one shell hole plainly showing under the bridge and on the waterline, also the destroyer *Attack* making for us.

I stood by the guard rails which were down, and saw the Admiral was going to jump on board. I stood by to steady him but it wasn't necessary. As soon as he was on board he was surrounded by men who ran to the spot and with cries of 'Good old David' and slapping him on the back he had to fight his way through them and ran forward to the Bridge to try to make contact with the enemy, still followed by shouts of Good old David; and that was the name he was known by on the Mess Decks: 'Good old David.'

As the year 1915 staggered out, with no sign of the enemy since Dogger Bank in January, the Fleet became sadly inured to incessant and fruitless sweeps in dreadful weather, 'During December fog or mist were experienced at Scapa on the 15th, 22nd, 25th and 26th; gales on the 6th, 8th and 23rd; and snow on the 3rd, 4th, 8th and 12th.'[1] When Beatty called it 'a desolate place: even the midshipmen are depressed,' there was summertime. The general gloom deepened with news of stalemate on land, but 'the bees of hell' were increasingly busy and by April had 'stored their hives' in a network of trenches, intricate as the streets of a town, and stretching from Switzerland to the sea.

In one sector of the front line, held by Canadians, Charles Beatty was making a personal reconnaissance when he was buried by a shell-burst. Dug out of the crater, he refused to retire to A.D.S. (Advanced Dressing Station) until he had made his report, despite a shattered arm which later had to be amputated. His message survives, not on an official form but in pencil on a scrap of flimsy. It is as neat as it is legible, the handwriting rather boyish. Only the signature is shaky:—

General Harington Headquarters Can Corps
Have traced trench running between P2 and P3 up to communication trench which runs from P4. Am satisfied from what I saw we are holding positions pointed out to me by you this morning. Bombers are being relieved. Did wonderfully well. Went through Comm trench from P4 to about a hundred yards beyond crater. Do not think any Germans found point 64 to Piccadilly (?) forum and south of it in their old front line.

Charles Beatty
H.Q. Canadian (?)

[1] Being so far north, there was but little daylight in mid-winter anyway. The quotation is from Jellicoe op. cit., p. 263.

The question marks indicate illegible words. On the back of the paper, in Lu's precise hand, is written, 'St Eloi 2nd April 1916. Signed by Charles Beatty after being severely wounded'.

At a time when it was popularly supposed that the 'gilded Staff' spent most of their time drinking whisky behind the lines, this incident provides an antidote; for there was an *aide de camp* of the Commander of the Canadian Expeditionary Force creeping about in the mud at the front when he could have been with his horses, well back. Indeed, he had brought two of his own hunters over to France, for although the Canadians were infantry, the role of an A.D.C. was still mounted, as it had been in the South African War when General Alderson so much appreciated his services that in his oddly titled book '*Foxhunting as a Guide to Soldiering*,' of which Charles had a presentation copy, he wrote 'To the best Galloper that ever General had.'

Now that Charles was out of the war, his loss was noted in high places:—

Buckingham Palace

Lt. Gen.   8th April 1916
Sir E. A. H. Alderson K.C.B.
Headquarters Canadian Corps.

My dear General,

The King was indeed distressed to hear that Beatty had been wounded, and had to lose his left arm. His Majesty noticed his name in the Casualty List two days ago, and instructed me to enquire about his wounds. We were unable to get any information about him yesterday, and your letter has arrived most opportunely.

The King knows that he will be a great loss to you, and His Majesty was only yesterday recalling the incident when he cantered alongside the King's motor on a very handsome horse.

Should you see Beatty, will you please tell him from the King how truly His Majesty sympathises with him in his misfortune.

Would you also let me know to what hospital in England he may be sent, as I am sure His Majesty will take an early opportunity of visiting him.

Under the Royal Arms in scarlet the body of the letter is typed, but the subscription, 'Yours sincerely Clive Wigram' (the King's principal private secretary) is handwritten.

So Charles came back to London, out of the war for good, whence, after operations, he returned to Borodale where, by a bizarre accident, he received further injury to what little was left of his arm. It would be the death of him.

At this time, early May, so strong was the feeling that the German High Seas Fleet was about to seek action, that the Government took the extraordinary step of sending war correspondents to the Firth of Forth and Scapa Flow, despite the Navy's marked aversion to publicity; summed up by David with, 'I don't like it. I don't want it. And I won't have it!' One of these newspapermen[1] has left an enduring picture of both Jellicoe and Beatty, whom he interviewed on board their respective flagships. . . .

'Jellicoe tight-lipped in what might have been a drawing-room except for a large chart on the wall by the fireplace. Could this be a battleship? It was so peaceful and homelike. There were easy chairs and a divan covered in flowered chintz. French windows opened onto a stern walk bright with potted geraniums. I was astonished to see in one corner a baby grand piano with open keyboard and loose sheets of music on its rack. A silver framed photograph of Lady Jellicoe stood on the flat top. Near a divan chair was a revolving bookcase. A large carpet, curtained windows and a log fire burning in the open grate, completed the domestic scene. . . Admiral Jellicoe himself, apart from the heavy gold lace on his sleeves and his ribbon decorations contributed to the illusion. (Of the indestructibility of such great ships.) Sturdy, medium in height, with a smiling round face and twinkling eyes, in other garb he might have been a country vicar like his brother. He had nothing of Beatty's leonine appearance, but we knew of an incisiveness which belied his amiable appearance. He had the reputation of being a quick worker who never showed any temper.'

[1] Roberts (C): *The Years of Promise* (Hodder 1968).

Above The King and Prince of Wales at Rosyth before the surrender of the German Navy
Below H.M.S. *Lion*

Above left Beatty at the Priory, Reigate
Above right Vice Admiral Sir David Beatty commanding the first battle-cruiser squadron
Below The Admiral in July 1919

Above Roehampton, May 1921
Below Wedding of Lord Louis Mountbatten, July 1922

Above Beatty inspecting Guard of Honour at Unveiling of the Exeter War Memorial,
July 1923
Below Armistice Day, 1923

Above left Beatty and his son Lord Borodale at the Army Point-to-Point in Gloucestershire, 1926
Above right Earl and Lady Beatty at Ascot, 1925
Below Beatty and Major Courage at Hurlingham, 1921

Above left Opening of the Hunting Season at Godstow Green
Below left Lord Westmorland and Beatty, 1925
Right The Admiral in Brussels, 1922

Above Bronze bust in Trafalgar Square
Below Borodale House in 1931 and after demolition in 1935

Earl Beatty

The foregoing accurate description tallies with everything written about Jellicoe but omits perhaps his most exceptional ability: calculation of complex risks such as only the Commander of a gigantic fleet is faced with. He also had a power of resolute action, in pursuit of his decisions, regardless of whether it was popular or abhorrent. The drawing-room effect was the rule rather than exception, though Beatty had simpler tastes. Perhaps both men took their cue for decoration from *Enchantress*, the Admiralty yacht, in which the main room – it were absurd to call it a cabin – was furnished like a West End Club, though with flowered chintz on the chairs instead of conventional leather.

On 14th May the war correspondents visited the battle cruisers in the Firth of Forth and interviewed their commander . . .

'There we met the now legendary figure, Vice-Admiral Sir David Beatty. He was to be the last spectacular figure in British naval history. Never again would the Service touch such a height of power and glory. It was fitting that Beatty should fly his flag in the *Lion*. He was a lion of a man with his handsome, strong-jawed face, his bulldog air and his habit of wearing his peaked Admiral's cap at a rakish angle. He was the perfect image of the public's idea of a daring sea-dog in the Drake tradition. His postcard photo was in every newsagent's window. The Press built him up. He came of horsey Irish stock, hence his hunting-box in Leicestershire and his constant riding to hounds. He married a Chicago store tycoon's daughter, a divorcée. They lived in some state with a house in Grosvenor Square, a castle in Scotland, a yacht and a hunting-box,[1] Brooksby Hall, the ancestral home of the Villiers for five hundred years, and where the famous Duke of Buckingham was born. Beatty had something in common, a panache, with that Leicestershire lad in whose home he lived. Like Villiers he was *persona grata* at Court. Behind this spectacular façade was a man of very solid achievement and some sensational episodes in his march to fame. . . .

'He was very affable with us, talked freely to everyone. "I wish

---

[1] Roberts runs ahead. David and Ethel did have Brooksby and Hanover Lodge, with the yacht, but the days of spectacular grandeur were not yet, and he had no opportunity for hunting, or any other activities ashore which would take more than a few hours.

we could get at 'em. If only they'd come out!" How little any of us there that morning knew what was ahead within a week.'[1]

Though the contrast in build and bearing between the two Admirals was generally the first impression people received, no less striking was the similarity between the ways their minds worked: Jellicoe the superb strategist, Beatty the brilliant tactician. So well did their ideas and methods match that frequently each seemed to know what the other would do, even in circumstances which precluded normal means of communication. Nor was this compatibility due solely to long association, which had been growing even before those hazardous days in China. Despite their marked individuality they had been through the same mill, and were therefore of the same mould: a superior product which gave them entrée to the Navy's inner circle. An additional bond could have been mutual recognition that having so often cheated death already, they seemed to have charmed lives.

During the war correspondents' interview with Beatty someone had the temerity to put the most delicate of all questions: what was the Navy's assessment of our chances in fleet action? Most Officers would have been evasive or refused to answer, but, with deadly accuracy which must have shaken the whole group, Beatty retorted, 'If the German fleet gets wiped out it really loses little. If we get wiped out, we lose everything.' There, in the proverbial nutshell, is the essence of naval strategy 1914–18, an appreciation of the situation as understood and applied by both senior Admirals.

Just sixteen days after the incident, on 30th May, the whole of the Grand Fleet began yet another sweep in the hope of enticing the enemy to quit his bases with the object of cutting off a portion of our forces, destroying it, and returning home before retribution could catch up. The Battle Cruiser Fleet left the Firth of Forth, to steer east across the hundred and twenty thousand square miles of the North Sea and rendezvous with the Dreadnought Battle Fleet at two o'clock on the following afternoon, off Denmark's west coat. The combined forces, though separated by some miles, would then proceed to the Skagerrack, between Norway and Denmark.

[1] Roberts underestimates. He must refer to Jutland but that would still be 17 days ahead, not a week.

At two o'clock next afternoon, the thirty-first, the junction was effected, with Jellicoe some ten miles astern of Beatty:—

'Even in the fleet flagship there was no indication that this was to be anything but yet another abortive sweep. Except for the one indecipherable signal "31 Gg 2490" there were no indications that the German fleet was putting to sea. From wireless call-signs, Sheer's flagship was still placed in the Jade. The fact that it was the usual German practice to transfer the call-sign to the shore signal station on going to sea had been overlooked by the Admiralty's interception services.'[1]

A quarter of an hour later the battle cruisers and attached, fifth, battle squadron – replacing three battle cruisers which had been detached previously for gunnery practice – having reached the eastward limit of the sweep, turned northward, towards Jellicoe. It looked like another failure to come to grips, but, over the horizon to the north-east, fate, in the unlikely guise of a small neutral steamer, was about to enter the arena. It had just been sighted by advanced elements of the enemy, and Vice-Admiral von Hipper, commanding the German battle cruiser force, detached the destroyer *Elbing* to investigate. At the same time two British light cruisers were accidentally converging from the opposite direction. When they sighted the neutral she was hove-to for routine inspection, as practiced by both sides in search of contraband. Recognition was instantaneous. Both sides broke wireless silence with 'Enemy in sight,' and a few minutes later the light cruiser *Galatea* fired the first round in the epic contest which, but for the merest chance, might never have occurred through the whole length of the war.

'After receiving reports of enemy in sight from *Galatea*, Vice-Admiral Beatty ordered H.M.S. *Engadine*, a seaplane carrier accompanying the battle cruiser force, to send up a seaplane to reconnoitre, and at 3.8 p.m. a two-seater "Short" seaplane with a 225 h.p. Sunbeam engine flew off the water with Assistant Pay-master G. S. Trewin as Observer and Flight-Lieutenant F. R. Rutland as Pilot. "The picture from the air," says one of these

---

[1] Macintyre (D): *Jutland* (Evans 1957) The signal was in fact the executive order from Admiral Sheer, Commander in Chief of the High Seas Fleet, to proceed with a major sortie of the kind expected by the British.

officers, "of the battle cruisers and of the Queen Elizabeth class battleships (5th battle squadron) with their attendant light cruiser screen and destroyers, all rushing forward in what may be termed an orderly helter-skelter in a south-westerly direction in order to cut off the enemy, is a picture that can never be forgotten".[1]

Those two officers, who gallantly flew low through smoke and gunfire to identify enemy ships, and then reported to Beatty by wireless, made history that day. Never before had an aeroplane been used for 'spotting' at sea.

So, from this simple encounter there rapidly developed a conflict of increasing complexity, the like of which could not have been anticipated by either side, because such conditions could not have been contrived on manoeuvres. Only with the greatest difficulty would the rival Admirals be able to keep even a semblance of control over the *melée*, while communications became more and more difficult. Though the weather was good, the sea calm – if it had not been the seaplane would not have been able to take off – changing visibility confused every tactical situation as it developed; until not even Jellicoe knew where many of his squadrons were or what course they were steering. Beatty in this respect was better placed, for his tactics as laid down were to engage enemy battle cruisers and lead them towards the Grand Fleet for execution. The time was now 4.40 p.m. and as yet Hipper had no idea that the Grand Fleet was at sea.

That Jellicoe's plan was successful probably saved Beatty from a local defeat, despite the additional power of the Fifth Battle Squadron, representing the most modern and powerful capital ships afloat; in that the action with Hipper went disastrously against him; due to structural and design weaknesses in his apparently indestructible vessels. Nor was his own fire as effective as it should have been, because of ineffective armour-piercing shells. Within twenty minutes, two battle cruisers, *Indefatigable* and *Queen Mary*, were blown to bits, with the loss of almost their entire complements. This left him numerically inferior as well as in terms of fire-power. Two hours later *Invincible* likewise disappeared, in a matter of seconds, and *Lion*, already badly hurt,

[1] Extract from *The Fighting at Jutland* (Personal Experiences) privately printed 1921.

survived only through the gallantry of Major F. J. H. Harvey, Royal Marine Light Infantry, who, mortally wounded, from his wrecked turret ordered the flooding of its magazines. He was awarded a posthumous V.C.

Whether Beatty felt the hand of destiny, or that *le bon Dieu* was keeping an eye on him, his unshakeable composure under these appalling conditions was almost superhuman. When there was nothing floating where a few minutes before *Invincible* had been in action, he remarked to Chatfield, his Flag Captain, 'Seems to be something wrong with our bloody ships today.' The *Lion* signalled the rest of the Force, 'Port two points' – towards the enemy.

Captain Donald Macintyre, D.S.O. and two bars, wrote in his book, *Jutland*, of this incident, 'The very completeness and suddenness of *Invincible*'s destruction could not but have a shattering effect on the morale of all who saw it.' Yet the subsequent course of the action shows that, from the Admiral down to Boy First Class, Jack Cornwell ($16\frac{1}{2}$), also awarded a posthumous V.C., morale was not only resilient. It effectively rose, along with the long-cherished hope for a decisive victory.

Heavily damaged and with fires raging, the remaining battle cruisers continued on course and in station, until, according to plan, they swept aside to allow the Grand Fleet to fall upon the High Seas Fleet, now coming up in the wake of the enemy battle cruiser force. The battleships opened fire at a range of ten miles, and, as one German witness described the scene, 'It was as though the whole horizon was a line of belching guns.' Meanwhile among Beatty's ships and the lighter vessels in company with them the change of course had resulted in a most confused and dangerous situation, subsequently termed 'Windy Corner'.

'The scene will never be forgotten by those privileged to have witnessed it: with the fleet deploying, the rear divisions opening fire, *Defence* blowing up, *Warspite* turning in circles enveloped in shell-splashes, *Warrior* limping through them, and a seeming jumble of ships of all classes hurrying eastward, pressing past *Lion*'s battle cruisers who were still firing heavily as they faded into the mist; the intervening water-space was torn with shell splashes and the seamanship displayed was of an order beyond description. . . . As seen from the Fifth Battle Squadron, turning up at the rear of the battle line, "the general effect outdid the most imaginative picture of a naval battle".[1]

In the increasing murk it became more and more difficult for individual ships to know quite where they were, still less what others were doing, and fleet commanders were starved of information because wireless aerials were shot away, lamps and flags difficult, if not impossible, to read. It was under these circumstances that the whole German Fleet managed to extricate itself from the closing trap, but so desperate was their plight that Hipper ordered his remaining battle cruisers to 'Charge!' and 'Ram!' in the hope that they would at least delay the oncoming horde. There were only four of them left and all severely damaged, yet they turned back, on what the Germans later described as their 'Death Ride'; as certainly it would have been had not Vice-Admiral Sheer, Commander-in-Chief, relying on a massed attack by lighter craft, countermanded the order before contact was made. The time was 7.20 p.m., and there was still plenty of light to finish off the High Seas Fleet, now running westwards in confusion. Or so it seemed; but the enemy torpedo attack was pressed home with such vigour that Jellicoe was forced to give way. No doubt he was confident that, as the attacking destroyers retired, having loosed their torpedoes, he could soon re-establish his command of the whole operation; but it did not work out that way. Between bad visibility and lack of communications the two fleets began to diverge . . . 'Jellicoe, the torpedo attack disposed of, turned to a course which, in fact continued to take the two fleets further apart, and awaited clarification of the situation. The sands of opportunity were fast running out.'[2]

Shortly before eight o'clock the two fleets were again converging, and Beatty signalled, in cypher, to Jellicoe, 'Submit van of battleships follow battle cruisers. We can then cut off the whole of the enemy's battle fleet.' To this day nobody knows on what grounds that confident prediction was made; but in the nature of the man it must have been done on a seeming certainty, and had it come off there would indeed have been a Trafalgar, instead of an anticlimax. Jellicoe could not 'follow battle cruisers' because he

---

[1] Irving (J): *The Smoke Screen of Jutland* (Kimber 1966) Commander John Irving R.N.).
[2] Irving op.cit.

did not know where they were, or on what course; and Beatty must have lost touch with the enemy while Jellicoe was trying to piece together what little information he had that was even vaguely reliable. Both Admirals, however, remained convinced that the enemy was in open water to the West. It therefore seemed proper to dispose Battle Cruiser Force and Grand Fleet for night stations: on two assumptions, both of which were false. The first was that, come daylight, the British would be between the Germans and their base. The second, equally disastrous, was that it was impractical for the High Seas Fleet to attempt to break through the massive British lines in the dark. But it did, and by four o'clock next morning the Admiralty informed Jellicoe that the enemy was back in harbour.

In all this confusion the lack of communications is critical, and the enemy were just as ill informed as ourselves, or even more so. The surprising thing is not that confusion reigned from early afternoon on the 30th May till the small hours of the 1st June, it is that *despite* dearth of vital intelligence the order and management of those tremendous squadrons went like an exercise. What did not, was the operations room at the Admiralty, which failed to pass to Jellicoe no less than seven intercepted German signals to the High Seas Fleet which clearly defined their intentions, track and positions: aiming for the Horns Reef passage to the mouth of the River Jade and their base. The first of these was made by Admiral Scheer at 10.32 p.m., the last at 1.03 a.m.

'By 1 a.m. on 1st June, Jellicoe, had this information reached him, could have called upon Beatty and his battle cruisers to follow him, and, ordering his destroyers to join him, turned eastward with his battle fleet at twenty knots; he could have been ready and waiting, in line of battle, between the entrance to the swept channel and Scheer's rendezvous, off Horns Reef. It would by then have been light enough for the British gunlayers to have seen Scheer's battered and somewhat disorganised fleet; there would have been seventeen hours of daylight in which to finish the business in hand. Once more the date would have been a great naval occasion – another 'glorious First of June.'[1]

The above quotation is also from Commander Irving's book,

---

[1] A reference to Lord Howes victory over the combined Spanish and French fleets in 1793.

which attributes the failure of the Admiralty to pass on those signals to jealousy between the civilian experts in the cypher room – for we had broken the German code early in the war – and the executive officers next door. To a layman it seems incredible that such a state of affairs could have existed to the point where the Director Naval Operations would, out of spite, suppress signals, passed to him decoded, upon which might depend the outcome of the battle. Moreover, were such a thing proven, the executive officers responsible must surely have been court-martialled. There is, happily, a more probable explanation which hardly merits a charge of dereliction of duty, still less of treachery. All through this action there were communications problems, unique problems; but the Admiralty could no more have anticipated this than did the Admirals. Instead they would have assumed, as did the Admirals, that the elaborate signalling systems which had, apparently, been perfected during endless exercises, would be sufficient to keep the Commander-in-Chief fully informed, not only of his own dispositions but also those of the enemy.

That being so, the Admiralty would also have assumed that Jellicoe, from local sources, would have at least as much knowledge of the enemy's movements, and probably more. Indeed, it might even have happened that a duty officer decided not to add to Jellicoe's burden by overloading his wireless channels with information emanating from the shore-based German Headquarters; information which at best would tell the Admiral what he knew already, and at worst would confuse him.

Space wars may come upon us, and global conflicts with weapons unimaginable, but the Battle of Jutland will remain unprecedented and unequalled in the history of warships. The spirit in which they were fought, on both sides, will endure as a monument to heroism in the line of duty. It may also remain unique as the last time Admirals directed their fleets from the open bridge, and this is particularly the case with the battle cruisers, Vice-Admiral von Hipper, commanding First Scouting Group, opposed Sir David Beatty of the Battle Cruiser Fleet[1] in a personal

[1] Fleet and Force are used by some writers as equivalent terms. Properly speaking Force refers to the battle cruiser squadrons themselves, and Fleet includes all ancillary vessels, cruisers, light cruisers and destroyers.

contest of will and wits, complex as any match between chess masters yet conducted in total uproar and mortal danger. Confusion was everywhere around them. Control of their ships depended largely upon inspired guesswork.

Even through the dry details of official communications one can smell cordite. As for the controversy about Beatty's tactics, if anyone still wants an authoritative account, to whom should he turn except Jellicoe? Our Admiral himself was content with his superior's judgement and never published anything on his own behalf. Furthermore, Jellicoe approved *in toto* Beatty's depatch concerned with the battle cruisers and their numerous ancillary vessels. Here are a few short excerpts from Jellicoe's definitive work *The Grand Fleet 1914–1916*.

BATTLE OF JUTLAND DESPATCH[1]

No. 1395 H.F. 0022   *Iron Duke*
18th June 1916

The Secretary of the Admiralty

Sir, –
Be pleased to inform the Lords Commissioners of the Admiralty that the German High Seas Fleet was brought to action on 31st May, 1916, to the westward of the Jutland Bank off the coast of Denmark.

2. The available ships of the Grand Fleet in pursuance of the general policy of periodical sweeps through the North Sea, had left its bases on the previous day, in accordance with instructions issued by me.

3. The ships under my command taking part in the sweep were as follows:
    (a) Those in company with me.
(There follows a list of ninety-nine vessels. At Trafalgar, Nelson deployed twenty-seven.)

---

[1] The Despatch forms Appendix 1 of the book and occupies twenty-nine pages, including a separate section under the heading: The Battle Cruisers in the Van. In all there are thirty-six paragraphs of which the above is of course the first and the only one without a numeral.

(b) Those in company with Vice-Admiral Sir David Beatty. (There follows a list of fifty-two vessels, giving a total of a hundred and fifty-one. With the enemy it was much the same. Though short on heavy ships they had more destroyers, so that from noon on 31st May to dawn on 1st June more than two hundred men-o'-war were raging. How they were kept under control passes imagination.)

16. Battle Cruisers in the van. Sir David Beatty reports. (There follow several quotations from Beatty's report, inserted so as to give a coherent narrative of the entire complex action, each incident accurately timed. Both admirals pay tribute to an overriding spirit.)

(Jellicoe continued)

The conduct of officers and men throughout the day and night actions was entirely beyond praise. No words of mine could do them justice. On all sides it was reported to me that the glorious traditions of the past were most worthily upheld – whether in heavy ships, cruisers, light cruisers or destroyers – the same indefatigable spirit prevailed. Officers and men were cool and determined, with a cheeriness that would have carried them through anything. The heroism of the wounded was the admiration of all.

I cannot adequately express the pride with which the spirit of the Fleet filled me.

(Beatty quoted by Jellicoe)

Shortly after 4 p.m. *Indefatigable*, after a violent explosion, fell out of the line, turned over and sank . . .

At 4.26 p.m. there was a violent explosion in *Queen Mary*; she was enveloped in clouds of grey smoke and disappeared. Eighteen of her officers and men were subsequently picked up by *Laurel* . . .

At 6.33 p.m. *Invincible* blew up.

(Jellicoe continued: end of his despatch)

Sir David Beatty once again showed his fine qualities of gallant leadership, firm determination and correct strategic insight . . . The services rendered by him, not only on this, but on two previous occasions, have been of the very greatest value . . .

36. In a separate despatch I propose to bring to the notice of their Lordships the names of other officers and men who did not come under my personal observation, but who had the opportunity of specially distinguishing themselves.

I am, Sir,

Your obedient servant

(signed) J R Jellicoe

Admiral, Commander-in-Chief

Not only is the Despatch incontrovertible, so is his appreciation of the detailed activity of the Fleet from the outbreak of war until he relinquished command; to be succeeded by Beatty. His book is meticulously written and supported by many charts, sketches and tables. It appeared in 1919 after he had access to the German records. They emphasised the strategic role of a fleet in being and showed how their ships differed from ours to their considerable advantage. For instance, because of the Empire ours were designed for prolonged sea-keeping in any climate. Theirs were built for little more than excursions into the Baltic or the North Sea. Consequently there was a great saving in bulk and crews' quarters, permitting heavier armour and allowing more space for machinery of all kinds. Because a ship's complement based on Kiel spent much of their time in barracks there was also an advantage in terms of maintenance and morale.

Because until the end of the war we could not know about these matters the discrepancies between British and German versions of any particular action could not be reconciled. Hence the controversy. We did not know for instance that our shells often failed to penetrate but knew, only too well, that theirs, plunging, went through hulls and decks more thoroughly than had been thought possible.

On the 18th August 1916 the German Headquarters showed unusual activity. A stream of signals to the High Seas Fleet was intercepted and decoded at the Admiralty, though, as usual, there was no mention of the specific objective; which would be known only to Admirals and Captains through written orders. Only after the war did the German Official history reveal it:—

95

'To bombard Sunderland (on England's north-east coast), to force the English fleet to come out, and show the world the unbroken strength of the German fleet.'

An unusual grouping of submarines confirmed the impression that a major excursion was imminent, 'Everybody was certain there was going to be an action. The Commander-in-Chief and Beatty were quite sure. I was on the bridge at the time (morning of the 19th) attending on the Captain (Chatfield of *Lion*) and he told me to report to the engine room, "We will probably be opening fire in fifteen or twenty minutes." We sighted five or six Zeppelins, who gave us away and prevented any action. Our seaplane carrier sent up a seaplane and one of our light cruisers opened fire. Five minutes after going off watch one of our screen, the *Nottingham*, was "mouldied" (torpedoed) and on our return the *Lowestoft* went up, (another of our screen) about ten minutes before I went on watch. We had three "mouldies" miss us on the way back and every B.C. (battle cruiser) had two or three fired at them.'

Later, the *Lion* heeled hard over while the midshipmen were having tea in the gunroom, and they all rushed up on deck, 'to find we were in the middle of a minefield laid for our benefit, and while we were still altering course to avoid mines a torpedo was fired that missed us by a matter of feet.'

Midshipman Mountbatten had missed Jutland because he was in hospital with a broken leg and had joined *Lion* only a few days before he wrote the letter from which the above quotation comes.[1] His clarity of expression matches his accurate observation, and both fully bear out Jellicoe's emphasis on the torpedo menace, for which he would be unfairly charged with undue caution. By this period of the war it would be quite feasible for the Germans to gain a decisive advantage over the Grand Fleet without firing a gun.

A unique feature of the abortive action was the number of airships employed, at least ten, flying too high to be reached by gunfire and forming a screen from which virtually the whole of the critical part of England's coastline could be observed. So

---

[1] Letter from Midshipman 'Dickie' Mountbatten, later Admiral Earl Mountbatten of Burma dated 27th May 1917. Quoted in Richard Hough's *The Mountbattens*, pp. 318, 319.

elaborate were the German dispositions that Jellicoe thought that instead of being just another tip-and-run raid it might be the cover for an invasion force. The enemy never again appeared in Fleet formation until they staged, in 1918, an abortive attempt on a convoy which they did not even locate. By then the crews were mutinous.

At the end of October Jellicoe handed over the supreme command to Beatty, who tactfully hoisted his flag, not in *Iron Duke* but *Queen Elizabeth*. This change of command has often been interpreted as a demotion for Jellicoe, and a reward for Beatty on account of his conduct at Jutland; but here, in his own words, is how the retiring Commander-in-Chief saw the situation. Does he sound like one who has been dismissed?

'On November 1st I left *Iron Duke* at Cromarty and proceeded to the Admiralty at the request of the First Lord, Mr Balfour. The visit was the result of letters I had written on the subject of the evergrowing danger of the submarine to our sea communications, and the necessity for the adoption of the most energetic measures to deal with this danger. It had been for some time my opinion that unless the Navy could devise effective means, first to destroy the submarines, and, second, to protect our communications more successfully until the submarines could be destroyed, there was an undoubted risk of our being forced into an unsatisfactory peace . . . I knew that the First Sea Lord, Sir Henry Jackson, was alive to this danger, and that it caused him much anxiety. We had corresponded very freely on all subjects during his tenure of office at the Admiralty, and I was aware of his view on the subject of war policy, on which we had always been in complete agreement.'

By this masterly analysis, with appropriate emphasis on understatement, he completely demolishes any idea that in leaving the Grand Fleet he was being demoted. Indeed, as First Sea Lord he would still be senior to Beatty, and his responsibilities greater.

Though at the Admiralty he could not 'lose the war in an afternoon,' failure to beat the submarines would, if slowly, also have lost us the war. To conclude this honourable comparison, had there been any difference of opinion between Jellicoe and Beatty, then it would soon have been demonstrated by altered tactics, and perhaps strategy. In fact there were no major changes of any kind. This particularly applies to underwater attack other than by submarines; for there was no escaping the constant threat from mines (moored, floating or drifting), from the submerged torpedo tubes of capital ships, and from the deck-tubes of destroyers.

Of this problem Jellicoe had made a special study and communicated his finding soon after accepting supreme command. He did so in courageous recognition that he would be taunted by those who remained unaware that it was no longer enough for Britannia to rule the waves. She must also control the depths. His forebodings were fully borne out. Both inside and outside the Service, the vast majority still thought that the capital ship reigned supreme. On 14th October 1914 he summarised this demonstration of moral courage in a letter to the Admiralty:—

'I feel that such (cautious) tactics, if not understood, may bring odium upon me. It is quite within the bounds of possibility that half our battle fleet might be disabled by underwater attack before the guns opened fire at all.'

Even with the all-out efforts of both Admirals, had America not entered the war in the following year, 1917, and promptly strengthened the anti-submarine endeavour, it is probable that Britain would have been starved into submission. What irony that the historic decision, made on the personal initiative of President Wilson against those Isolationists whose policy was still to let Europe stew in her own blood, was a direct consequence of the strategic victory of Jutland! The Kaiser unleashed 'unrestricted submarine warfare', even against United States shipping, because of being forced to abandon hope of ever again challenging the Royal Navy to a major combat. The idea that the High Seas Fleet might at least, through tip-and-run tactics, ease the stronghold of the blockade, also had to be discarded; for virtually all the mercantile marine of the Central Powers was lying useless in harbour.

Nor is this the only way in which Jutland, though in terms of battle inconclusive, produced tremendous effects. Had the longed-for new Trafalgar been achieved, it is highly improbable that America would have come in; for opinion would certainly have turned against Wilson, particularly if, as would surely have happened, Germany exempted U.S. shipping from the underwater offensive. It is true, of course, that with the destruction of the High Seas Fleet many more units could have been deployed against the underwater menace; but intensification of the counter-blockade would have gone on. Nor would a new Trafalgar have had any effect on the armies. The conclusion, therefore, seems unavoidable that a decisive naval victory would have lost us the war, but a tactical defeat won it.

As to the relative stature of Jellicoe and Beatty, the concensus of opinions – and there are many – amounts to this: though temperamentally different, as Commanders they were much the same. It was pointless to marshal evidence for and against either when unassailable witnesses accept them as equals. Call Winston Churchill and Sir Henry Newbolt:—

'It might fall to him (Jellicoe) as to no other man, Sovereign, Statesman, Admiral or General, to issue orders which in the space of two or three hours might nakedly decide who won the war. The destruction of the British Fleet was final. He was the only man on either side who could lose the war in an afternoon. . . .

He (Beatty) was like Nelson pacing the bridge among shell fragments rebounding from the water.

The movement of their (both Admirals) blind, inanimate castles of steel was governed entirely by the will of a single man.'

(*World Crisis* 112 ff)

'It was a burden in itself great beyond all experience, and since the contest and the hazard were on a Titanic scale, the anxieties of these high officers were even more exhausting than their incessant labours.'

(Newbolt: *Naval Ops.*)

Relevant to the burden of anxiety, both Jellicoe and Hipper suffered from nervous exhaustion, and, although he never admits it, one can hardly claim Beatty to have been superhuman in this respect. The amazing fact is that none of these men, and one may add Sheer as Jellicoe's opposite number, ever in any important respect failed not only to rise to an occasion, nor to retain the confidence of those under their command. Of Jellicoe, His Majesty King George V, said, in an address on board the flagship after Jutland:—

'Sir John Jellicoe, officers and men of the Grand Fleet, you have waited for nearly two years with most exemplary patience for the opportunity of meeting and engaging the enemy's fleet.

I can well understand how trying has been this period, and how great must have been the relief when you knew on May 31st that the enemy had been sighted.

Unfavourable weather conditions and approaching darkness prevented that completed result which you all expected, but you did all that was possible in the circumstances. You drove the enemy into his harbours, and inflicted on him very severe losses, and you added yet another page to the glorious traditions of the British Navy.

You could not do more, and for your splendid work I thank you[1].'

Splendid work indeed it was. Perhaps even more extraordinary than the superb seamanship, everywhere evident, and on both sides, was the morale of all ranks. Admirals had no monopoly in self-control, beyond normal limits:—

'With her tattered ensign still flying the waters had closed over *Ardent* (a destroyer). Looking around him the Captain could see forty or fifty heads bobbing in the water; there was not much support for anyone, and the ships and fleets had moved on. Commander Marsden said: "I spoke to many of my men, and saw most of them die one by one. Not a man of them showed any fear of death, and there was not a murmur, or complaint, or cry for help from a single soul. Their joy was, and they talked about it to the end, that they and the *Ardent* had 'done their bit' as they put it. None of the men appeared to suffer at all: they just seemed to lie back and go to sleep . . ." I awoke to find the flotilla-leader *Marksman* close alongside me. I sang out for help and in reply got a reassuring shout: "You're all right, sir; we are coming!" '

Commander Irving, from which the above is quoted, ends his book, *The Smoke Screen of Jutland* thus:—

'What Captain Marsden had to say of *Ardent*'s crew might be said of all, on both sides, who did not return after this battle, but took their long last trick down on the Jutland Banks alongside the wreckage of the ships they had manned and fought: "All hands fought the ship with the utmost gallantry and in a most tenacious and determined manner until she sank beneath them, and then met their death in that composed and happy spirit that I am

[1] Jellicoe op. cit., p. 430.

convinced comes to all those who do their duty to the end. May they rest in peace".'

POSTSCRIPT TO JUTLAND

Despite all the sound and fury of the Battle of Jutland only one Dreadnaught, *Colossus*, was hit; with two killed. As the full complement of the battle fleet was 20,000 this represents a mere ·01% casualty rate, so, in the event, it was safer to be with them in the ravaged North Sea than almost anywhere else; but this in no way diminishes the feat of arms, for against that the Battle Cruisers lost almost half their crews, with three sunk and others damaged: the equivalent of three Army Divisions annihilated. Even this horror, in the midst of which Admiral Beatty remained apparently unmoved, to be appreciated fully needs further comparison.

British and German Battle Fleets were both designed for a main armament broadside of armour-piercing shells with a total weight in excess of a thousand tons, and between them they fired 4,000 rounds. Of these only 120 hits were recorded, and only 12 'caused serious damage'. From German sources it was learned that their calculation showed the percentage of hits to rounds fired to be only 3·33% and they credited the British with even less: 2·17%.

Not the arithmetic but the appalling racket imposed the terrific physical and mental strain of battle under those conditions. What with the howl of the wind, vibration of the hull, the continuous sound, as of many waterfalls, of shell splashes, masthead high; added to gunfire, smoke, fire, and the shriek 'like an express train' of projectiles streaking overhead, normal sensory response had to be inhibited by sheer will-power. Phenomenal self-control was required of everyone; from the stoker choked with coal-dust and only the double bottom of the hull under him, through every deck and rank to the lookout in his crow's nest. In officers it seems to have induced an almost trance-like state, for not only did they suppress emotional response to the brouhaha. They calmly went on making decisions, calculations, signals, records and in many cases retained effective executive command after being severely wounded. In addition, Admirals had to consider not only the state of their own ships, but also what everyone else was doing, or supposed to be doing, in a high-speed flux of death and destruction over which it was always difficult, and sometimes impossible, to appreciate what was really happening.

Absence of signals, or their inaccurate, misleading nature was the rule rather than the exception; in which respect Jutland differs from Dogger Bank where, being on a much smaller scale, the contest was under control from beginning to end. At Dogger there was little of 'the fog of war' through which commanders cannot see either what is happening or what to do. At Jutland it was thick, almost from first contact between capital ships, and became, for the British, impenetrable during the night. In this respect among so many others Jutland was unique among sea fights. Flags could not be read because of smoke, whether from funnels belching furnace gases or chemicals intended to obscure observation. Lamps were almost equally handicapped in daylight, and at night, more often than not, gave a ship's position away to the enemy without achieving efficient reception. Wireless telegraphy was at best primitive, at worst inaudible, even when correctly transmitted, either through faulty receivers, jamming (deliberate or otherwise) or through gunfire.

It may well be that, despite these technical shortcomings, Jellicoe might have received the intelligence needed to recoup his lost advantage, had destroyers, actually engaging enemy capital ships during the night, been able to get through to him the identity, course and speed of the enemy's capital ships:—

'Throughout the destroyer actions of the night, when the destroyers realised that they were in contact with considerable forces of the German fleet, signals had been passed to Jellicoe in *Iron Duke*, leading the Grand Fleet southwards. At least, signals had been made, but even as the Germans had the night dispositions,[1] so they had the wavelength of the destroyers and most effectively jammed any signals they made.'

Tragically, this vital information had not reached *Iron Duke* from any other source, including the Admiralty, which had decoded two signals between 9.06 and 10.32 p.m. either of which would have made renewed action at dawn inevitable. The last signal was absolutely conclusive since it requested Zeppelin

[1] The enemy also knew the challenge and response signals.

reconnaisance off Horn's Reef at first light. The significance is so obvious that had Jellicoe received only that particular signal, he would have had plenty of time to get between the enemy and his base next morning, with the whole of a long summer day to finish him off.

Being in the dark in both senses, Jellicoe had no choice but to make his night dispositions and proceed on dead reckoning, even then, if he learned the enemy's course and speed well before dawn he might still have renewed the battle. Nothing came through, not from any of his hundreds of ships, nor from the Admiralty. Then the Germans clinched the issue by decoding British signals, so that they knew precisely where the Grand Fleet was, and where it would be next day, well away to the West. All Scheer had to do was to reduce speed while the British passed him in the dark. This he did, and waited until there was nothing between him and safety except destroyers astern of the Grand Fleet, which in turn was behind the battle cruisers on the same course. To blast his way through those relatively puny vessels was like using gunners against archers, and though they fought back, in many desperate encounters at close ranges, many were sunk or wrecked.

Nevertheless, it was at Jutland that the destroyer 'came of age' in that it outgrew its restricted role as defender of the capital ship against torpedo boats. Over and over again, both battle fleets had to take evasive action when faced with destroyer attack; which had to be countered by their own destroyer screens. Writers naturally tend to emphasise the action of capital ships, and eulogise their admirals; but it can be argued that the greatest single factor in the balance of power at sea was the torpedo. If it were not so, why did both battle fleets invariably turn away when faced with a determined destroyer attack? And if that argument be allowed, then the officers and men of the Jutland flotillas could have claimed that without them the admirals would not, for long, have been able to direct their big ships – or even keep afloat.

7

NOT WITH A BANG

While Jutland was being fought Charles was convalescing at Atherstone, still seeming to feel the arm which was no longer there; for he tried to prop himself up in bed on that, left, side, with the result that he fell to the floor. In the autumn the family went to Borodale, and though there was hardly six inches of stump – insufficient for a prosthesis – he insisted on riding. One morning he failed to return and was found, hours later, hanging with the stump hooked over the top bar of a field-gate which he had tried to open from the saddle; but the horse shied and threw him onto the gate. This added trauma was so severe that he had to return to London for another operation, on 18th April 1917. It should have been a simple matter, but he died on the table.

David received the fell news in his Fleet Flagship *Queen Elizabeth*[1] at Scapa and immediately telegraphed:—

> Mrs Beatty care of Sir Alfred Fripp 19 Portland Place Ldn
> Courage dear Lu my heart goes out to you Thank God I saw him last month Remember we are only in this world for a short span the thought gives me comfort
> love
David

He then wrote a heartbreak letter to Ethel, who was herself

---

[1] She was absent from Jutland because Churchill wanted her 15″ guns in support of the Gallipoli landing. In any case Beatty would prefer not to appear to usurp Jellicoe's beloved *Iron Duke*.

writing to Lu, widowed for the second time, at forty-eight. Her son by the first marriage, Alan Langlands, had been killed on the same day as her brother-in-law, Noel Turner; an indication of the swathe of Officers who, as leaders of their men in trench warfare, were the first to fall, and whose casualties were therefore proportionately higher than those among other ranks.

David to Ethel:—
   'I have lost my truest and best friend and the world has lost the straightest and best gentleman in it.'
Ethel to Lu:— (from Aberdour House, Aberdour, Fife)
   'Lu dearest, I am sending you the King's telegram, sent to *David*. Would you like to keep it for little Charlie or shall I keep it for him? My thoughts are always with you these days. David is feeling it *terribly*. He really loved Charles. I feel if only I could be with him it would help – but alas it cannot *be*.'

Lu wanted a private funeral but was overruled by the War Office:—
   'Major Beatty was buried at Atherstone with full military honours. The band of the Royal Warwickshire Regt. to which Major Beatty was attached, attended. Among the mourners were the widow and Major Vandeleur Beatty. Admiral Sir David Beatty was unable to be present. A memorial service was held at St Agnes Church, Newmarket at the same time as the funeral at Atherstone. The Rev Colvil-Wallis, Rural Dean, officiated, and a number of racing folk were present.'[1]
   Although Jutland demonstrated the supremacy of the Royal Navy, neither Jellicoe nor Beatty expected the High Seas Fleet to come out again in force, but the likelihood of East Coast raids had increased because they could be carried out by detached squadrons and would be virtually impossible to intercept unless the Grand Fleet, or a substantial portion of it, was already at sea. This

[1] The V.C. and D.S.O. vol ii entry: Beatty, Major C. H. L. The first of the 3 vols has a Foreword by 'Admiral of the Fleet Earl Beatty, O.M., G.C.B., G.C.V.O., K.C.B.' Editor E. M. Humphries pub. The Standart Art Book Co Ltd c 1922.

problem was made more serious because the Admiralty was unpopular owing to their apparent failure to cope with the submarine menace. Consequently, regular sweeps continued and a method was devised to provide an early warning system based on our own submarines equipped with better wireless. On the 5th November 1916, just before Jellicoe handed over to his Second in Command, Sir Cecil Burney, one of these, on patrol off Horns Reef encountered four enemy battleships and managed to damage two of them with torpedoes. The squadron then retired, abandoning, no doubt, just such a raid as the Admirals had in mind.

On the 27th, Jellicoe was told by the First Lord (Mr Balfour) that Beatty had been chosen to succeed him,[1] and on the following day he said farewell to the ship's company of *Iron Duke* and proceeded to the Admiralty to take up the equally arduous duties of First Sea Lord, with special responsibility for anti-submarine measures and loyal co-operation from Beatty, who shared his priorities even though it meant detaching destroyers from the Grand Fleet.

Thus 1917 came in as the war's climacteric year, in which the burden on the Commander-in-Chief was greater than ever. Stalemate on land with appalling slaughter increased the depression which followed failure of the Dardanelles venture. Merchant ship losses continued to mount and still in the public mind the Navy seemed to be both arrogant and inept; an impression left by inadequate and inaccurate Press coverage after Jutland, which gave the Germans time to claim a victory before an adequate rebuttal appeared in British newspapers.

Then, one after another, new factors entered the death equation. Convoys were organised, escorted by destroyers. More British submarines of an improved type, came into service to strengthen the patrols. United States ships were sunk, and caused America to join the Allies, with immediate action in support of the transatlantic Merchant services. This, though it lessened some of the strain on Beatty, could not lift from his shoulders the awesome responsibility for assuring the safety of the American Expeditionary Force and its supplies. It was one thing to shepherd troops from Dover to Calais; quite another to sweep the wide ocean in such a way that should an enemy squadron, or even a

---

[1] The Commander-in-Chief is a 'full' Admiral.

single ship, slip through the net, it could be located and destroyed before getting a chance to wipe out crowded liners which, before the year's end, had transported, without loss, an American army. The original intention had been for United States troops to be seconded, in relatively small units, to suitable formations under Allied command, but, fortunately for them, General Pershing insisted on an independent command, and it was this which broke the back of the last German offensive in the following year, 1918. Victory was in sight.

Other trends in the gigantic struggle were pointing the same way. With the start of unrestricted submarine warfare further sorties by the High Seas Fleet had been forbidden on the Kaiser's order; and soon the morale of the crews, bored, and infected with revolutionary propaganda, fell to danger level. By midsummer 1917 there were branches of a secret Sailors' Union in every ship, their headquarters in the flagship *Friedrich der Grosse* which had fought so well at Skagerrak (Jutland) that Admiral Scheer was lauded as 'conqueror of the Grand Fleet'; for Germans still regarded the battle as *their* victory.

In a last effort to regain control through raising morale, the C-in-C High Seas Fleet, Admiral Reinhard Scheer ordered a sortie in April 1918, and at least succeeded in getting his turbulent crews to sail. The object was interception of a Norwegian convoy, its destruction to be effected before the British could reach the scene. He never found the convoy, partly due to fog, partly to inaccurate intelligence, and had to turn for home with morale lower than when he set out. Deterioration was everywhere evident in the ships themselves, even to the coal, which was so poor they could not make anything like full speed. In action that would be a grave handicap.

'Another four months and Scheer, like his old opponent, Jellicoe, struck his flag and took the post of Chief of Naval Staff, called, too late, to direct the Kaiser's naval strategy. The end was now near. As the Kaiser's Germany was falling into ruin, Scheer called for a last heroic gesture from the fleet, now in the hands of his trusted subordinate, Baron von Hipper. Demoralised as it was, this fleet would surely obey the gallant hero all Germany had acclaimed.

It was ordered to sea, but Hipper no longer controlled even his own flagship. Mutiny flared, and spread like a heath fire. The true reckoning of the effect of Jutland was now evident. A stoker was proclaimed by the Comrades as Hipper's successor in command, with the humiliated admiral as his assistant.'

Nothing could have destroyed Germany's sea power so effectively, not even annihilation, for, until the rot set in, her personnel had been superb, not only in terms of the legendary Teutonic discipline but also for competence and gallantry. Had every one of Scheer's ships gone to the bottom – and before they did they would have exacted heavy losses from the British – new ships and new crews would have replaced them. Now nothing would be heard of the High Seas Fleet until, in November, that is to say in another two months, it would be sailed by the soviets, their officers under duress, to surrender in the Firth of Forth. And it probably would *not* have sailed unless a rumour had been circulated that British ships were also flying the Red Flag.

Disaffection was by no means confined to the fleet. From end to end, the Fatherland was gripped by revolutionary ardour fuelled by the manifold privations which were the direct result of the blockade aggravated by a disastrous shortfall in the supply of agricultural produce, largely because of the indiscriminate call-up of farm workers. Little of this state of affairs was appreciated abroad. The blockade continued and so did the routine of 'sweeping' the sea; for although losses caused by U-Boats were much diminished there could be no relaxation. Added to the Commander-in-Chief's anxieties was the problem of how to deprive Germany of the ownership of her warships; for when a cease-fire came, the fact that they were still serviceable would constitute one of her few remaining assets.

The Armistice was signed at 6 a.m. on 11th November 1918 and became effective five hours later. The King immediately sent the following message to Beatty:—

'Now that the last and most formidable of our enemies has acknowledged the triumph of the Allied Armies on behalf of right and justice I wish to express my praise and thankfulness to the Officers and men and women of the Royal Navy and Marines and with their comrades with the Fleet Auxiliaries and Merchant Marine who for more than four years have kept open the seas, protected our shores, and given us safety ever since that fateful 4th

August 1914. I have remained steadfast in my confidence that whether Fortune frowned or smiled the Royal Navy would once more prove a sure shield of the British Empire in the hour of trial. Never in its history has the R.N. with God's help done greater things for us nor better maintained its whole glory. With grateful hearts the people of the British Empire value the white, red, and blue ensigns and those who have given their lives for the flag.

I am proud to have served in the Navy. I am prouder to be at its head on this memorable day.

George R.I.'

Signal
    12.50 p.m. from C-in-C Grand Fleet. General.
Armistice commenced at 1100 today, Monday, and the customary method in H.M. Service of celebrating an occasion is to be carried out by ships' companies, 'splicing the main brace at 1900 today. Hands are to make and mend clothes.'

The main brace was part of a windjammer's standing rigging. 'Make and mend' went back before Nelson's time when sailors had to do much of their own tailoring. The whole signal gradually came to mean 'time off', for the purpose of celebrating, with a double tot of rum: about half a pint of 98% proof spirit. Traditionally the signal is made only by the Monarch, at his expense.

That night, between nine thirty and ten o'clock, there was a spontaneous noisy demonstration throughout the fleet, with Very lights, sirens, and searchlights. Then the usual routine was resumed, for Germany was still the enemy and quite capable of hostilities in repudiation of the Allied Armistice Commission's terms; particularly, the naval provisions for which Beatty was responsible. They called for the internment of the High Seas Fleet in neutral ports, but, as was probably foreseen, the Allies failed to agree as to what ships should go where, so the Admiral on his own authority demanded that they all make for Rosyth, under guard. The only vessels to be left in German ports would be unseaworthy, and they must be inspected by the Commission to certify their disarmament.

To work out the complicated details of this colossal operation a preliminary conference was to be held, at which such matters as the order of sailing, courses, speeds, recognition signs, would be agreed; *after* formal acceptance by the German High Command, in the person of their politically appointed delegate, Admiral Hugo von Meurer, of the terms of the Armistice as it affected the two navies. The conference was held on the 15th of November, after H.M.S. *Oak* had met the light cruiser *Königsberg* at an agreed rendezvous to guide her through the British minefields:—

Signal
'9.50 p.m. Tees to Blyth for Submarines and British Grand Fleet Flotillas.
German cruiser *Konigsberg* flying illuminated ensign at gaff, burning lights at fore and main top, and navigation lights proceeding at 1800 from Straw for Firth of Forth at 21 knots. Acknowledge.'

After more than four years of navigating without lights the effect of such illuminations must have been the first actual experience, signals apart, that the war was indeed over. Yet trouble was on its way, from a quarter unsuspected by most people yet anticipated by the Admiral; because Naval Intelligence was aware that Communists were trying to set up an alternative government in Germany with executive power vested in Workers and Sailors Councils.

Königsberg signalled to C-in-C Grand Fleet that Admiral Meurer would be accompanied by Council delegates. This is the reply:—
'German Admiral should be informed that I am prepared to receive him immediately, but am not prepared to receive the Delegates of the Council.'

In the event, no one except Meurer and his staff of four was permitted to leave *Königsberg*, but that made no difference to their relations with the Soviet, which might repudiate any plan to which Meurer had pledged, not only the German High Command (Naval) but also the Central Government. It is extraordinary therefore that Meurer's officers, hitherto deprived even of their rank by the Soviet, not only retained the dignity of their calling, in the most humiliating circumstances. Somehow they managed to re-establish a command structure so that when the great surrender did take place it was conducted in an orderly and seamanlike manner – by mutineers. No credit seems to have been given to the German officers for this phenomenal achievement; for nothing is more difficult in terms of leadership than to regain authority after its basis: discipline and loyalty, has been destroyed. Credit is also due to their crews, for it must be almost as difficult for a mutineer to report for duty to the same authority which he had successfully defied.

Königsberg and *Oak*, her escort, anchored in fog that evening, 15th November, the former unaware that she was surrounded by great ships, which, though invisible, were the power behind the conference about to begin. The five German officers were brought alongside the flagship, *Queen Elizabeth*, in a picket boat, and were received with the customary punctilio on the brilliantly lit quarterdeck. They were then led past a Marine guard with fixed bayonets and conducted below, to the 'barn-like forecabin'[1] – Beatty's own phrase – which extended across the whole beam of the ship. There they confronted the Commander-in-Chief flanked by three staff officers on each side. Two other officers, wearing swords, faced them from chairs well back from the long table. Unnoticed, a distinguished artist in borrowed naval uniform, Sir John Lavery, stood at a side table, his sketch pads hidden behind a mass of flowers. How did they get to bleak Scapa in the middle of November?

Behind Beatty there hung on the bulkhead a full-length picture of Nelson, given him by Lu along with a Queen Anne silver tea-caddy which had been holed by a shell splinter at Jutland. On the table in front of him, and facing Meurer as he came in, was a nine inch brass doorstop, lead-filled, in the form of a crouching lion. The table itself, covered with a dark cloth which almost reached the floor, was strewn, in an orderly manner, with charts and miscellaneous papers. Lavery's picture shows the deck carpeted, the chairs white-painted, upholstered, and covered with striped fabric. Save for an apparently incongruous scuttle, it might have been the scene of a confrontation ashore.

The atmosphere was correct but cold. On being handed

---

[1] So called because it was forward of the Admiral's quarters in the stern, and not because it was 'forrad'.

Meurer's authority to negotiate, Beatty said, 'Pray be seated.' And that seems to have been the only remark of common courtesy which passed between them. Later, he described Meurer as 'ashen', and noted that on coming aboard he nearly collapsed. Ethel writing to Lu dwelt on his pitiful state, which, despite David's overt callousness, elicited his sympathy. For the plight of these enemy officers was worse that it could have been after defeat in battle. Though they represented authority at the highest level, on returning to *Königsberg* they would be virtually under arrest, stripped of all semblance of command.

With arrangements for the reception of the High Seas Fleet worked out in detail, Meurer broke away from the technical issues to utter a heartfelt plea, 'Would the blockade continue despite the Armistice? People were dropping dead in the streets from starvation, even women and children.' Beatty replied in the affirmative, though he must have realised such a decision was yet to be made, by the statesmen. He added, as though to leave no doubt but that the blockade would indeed continue, 'It is all your fault,' meaning that Germany had wrecked her own economy by persisting in a war of attrition.

The meeting did not break up until after midnight, and at 1.20 a.m. Admiral Meurer's long, signed statement of the terms was passed through the usual channels, 'as suggested by Commander-in-Chief Grand Fleet'. So passed the most critical hour since Jutland, midnight 15th/16th, Saturday November 1918; for until then, and even afterwards, there was a widespread belief that the conference would fail and probably incite the enemy to further hostilities, of which they were fully capable; provided, of course, that officers would be obeyed.

Meurer returned to *Königsberg* and then to Kiel. Beatty set about the detailed planning necessary to deploy his forces in such a way that any attempt at a last-minute suicidal action would be fruitless. He also had another, very different anxiety, for His Majesty George V was to pay a visit to the fleet only four days ahead, on the 20th; and this called for another set of contingency plans; particularly as he would be accompanied by Queen Mary and the Prince of Wales. The day was clear and fine, not marred by the least untoward incident. The royal party embarked in *Oak* at 11 a.m. and, preceded by H.M.S. *Verdun*, steamed majestically through the fleet, Royal Standard at the main and every ship they passed, manned by cheering sailors. Later, the King and the Prince went on board the American flagship *New York* – Admiral Rodman – before honouring *Lion* and *Revenge*. They had already, including the Queen, visited *Queen Elizabeth*, for luncheon. In addition to this taxing schedule she had toured the dockyard, inspected the Young Men's Christian Association recreational unit at Rosyth, and had tea on board H.M.S. *Revenge*. Nor was that the end of the day, for in the evening there was an official visit to Edinburgh which began when the Royal Train pulled in after a short run from Rosyth. They could not relax for a moment until, back in the train, they were on their way to London through the night. Simultaneously, the Grand Fleet was putting to sea, for the last time on a war footing.

From the journal of Commander Ouvry, then Lieutenant in the light cruiser *Inconstant*:—
'*Thursday 21st November 1918*
The Grand Fleet put to sea during the night to meet the portion of the German fleet for internment.

H.M.S. *Cardiff* (Flagship of the 6th light cruiser squadron, Admiral Alexander Sinclair) was detailed to lead in the German heavy ships. H.M.S. *Phaeton* (Captain Cameron,) 1st L.C.S. was to lead in the German light cruisers, and *Castor* (Commodore "F" Tweedie) the destroyers.

These three ships left harbour first, *Cardiff* towing a kite balloon for lookout purposes, and the whole of the Grand Fleet followed.

The first to sight the Germans was Commodore "F" in *Castor*.

The time for meeting the enemy was approximately 9.15 a.m. Accordingly ships companies were sent to action stations about 8.30 a.m.
Signal
Com "F" to *Cardiff*. Urgent.
Unknown number of suspicious vessels bearings 45 °E, steering west, 5 miles distant. My position 56°11' N 1° 25' W.
This was closely followed by:—
Signal
Unknown number of dreadnaught battleships in sight bearing S45°E, steering west distant 4 miles. My position 56° 11' N 2°. O.W.

The Germans should have been sighted bearing East, and as they were out for reckoning we had to move to the south eastward. This of course entailed a large number of signals and alterations of course. However, we finally got into position.

I had had the morning watch on *the* day, 4 a.m. until 7.30 a.m. during which time we had been steering S73°E at a speed from 10–12 knots. We passed May Island at 4.45 having weighed at 2 a.m. It seemed most extraordinary crawling along at 10 knots as of course previously we always steam about 20 knots at sea, also zigzag.

At 7.30 a.m. I went down and washed and had breakfast. At 8.30 a.m. "Action" was sounded and for the last time we all closed up seriously to our stations rigged in full war kit – gas masks, antiflash helmets, goggles, shrapnel helmets etc.

Having cleared away we settled down to meet the German ships, ready for action at a moment's notice . . .

Guns were not actually loaded but all ammunition was up and ready. Guns were trained fore and aft but Directors were kept laid "on" and ranges etc passed all ready for opening fire.

Steam was raised for "Full Speed".

The Squadron at the time was in Line Ahead, *Caledon* (R.A. Walter Cowan) leading. *Inconstant* being the rear ship.

I was up in the Fore Top with No. 1 (Acland, also a gunnery officer) and had the job of Asst "G" and Rate Officer.

It was quite a fine day, the sea being calm and the sun occasionally exhibiting itself. The visibility was only about 3 miles (6,000 yards). At 8.50 we sighted smoke on the starboard bow. The excitement was of course intense as it was impossible to tell whether the Hun had something up his sleeve for us or not. It seemed too wonderful for an extremely powerful fleet to give themselves up without a blow! One thing I do know – that if we had been in the position as those Hun we would have had a good run for *our* money before we got "put under".

Later though, when we found out that they had really had such a hammering at Jutland (which they claimed originally as a great victory for themselves) perhaps there is a little excuse for them having a fit of the "Blues", all the same when at 8.25 a.m. the smoke developed into a formation of German battle cruisers – looming out of the haze – we could hardly believe our eyes. *Cardiff* and *Seydlitz* were the first ships sighted. After the battle cruisers (5 in number) came 9 battleships led by *Friedrich der Grosse*, the German Fleet Flagship (2.0). Then came *Phaeton* followed by 7 German light cruisers (2.25) and lastly *Castor* followed by 49 German destroyers in 5 parallel lines (2.36).

No. 1 and myself clicked away with our cameras – without much hope as the light was so bad – at the same time, of course, keeping the (fire) control running in case of treachery.

We steamed past the whole line and at 9.45 turned 16 pts and reduced to 10 knots to keep station on the starboard quarter of the procession. The German destroyers, surrounded by our own were then on the port bow.

The Germans were under the following Admirals:—

Friedrich der Grosse, Rear-Admiral von Reuter

Seydlitz, Commodore Tagert

Karlsruhe, Commodore Harder

Rear-Admiral von Reuter was Senior Officer.

At 11.35 we "packed up" from Action Stations. Our one regret was that instead of *Nov* 21st it could have been *October* 21st, anniversary of Trafalgar.'

On arrival the German ships anchored off Inch Keith with a screen of Battleships and battle cruisers, and light cruisers round them anchored also. The following signals were received during Operation ZZ:—

8.35 a.m. Com 'F' to *Medina*

Are 50 destroyers present and are they all in one line?

8.35 a.m. *Cardiff* to C-in-C G.F.

Senior Officer reports he can only go 10 knots at present. Have reduced to 10.

8.51 a.m. C in C G.F. to SO light cruisers.

Report number of German light cruisers in company.

Reply seven.

The three ships of 1st L.C.S., *Inconstant*, *Galatea*, and *Royalist*, who were present, made the following signal to their Admiral (R. A. Cowan) in H.M.S. *Caledon* who was flying the silk flag presented to him by the Captains:—

'We are very proud that you should be flying silk flag this day, but wish it had the opportunity of gaining more scars like your ensign.'

Reply

'I thank you very much. I could never wish to go into action in better company, and the flag is a splendid reminder of you all that this is a sad day, though one of unequalled honour for our nation.'

At 10.40 a.m. The C-in-C made the following signal to the Admiralty:—

Signal

Grand Fleet met this morning at 09.30:—

5 Battle Cruisers

9 Battleships

7 Light Cruisers

and 49 Destroyers of the High Seas Fleet, which surrendered for internment, and are being brought to the Firth of Forth.

On arrival in the Firth of Forth, *Queen Elizabeth* with the C-in-C, Sir David Beatty, stopped, and the fleet steamed past, all ships massing their men on the forecastle and cheering him. The ships anchored outside Inch Keith as a guard to the surrendered German ships, and the remainder anchored in their old billets west of Inch Keith.

Thus closed what is, I am sure, one of the most dramatic incidents in the History of the Sea that the world has ever seen. 'Nothing can compare with the moment of sighting the 'Surrender' – which seemed incredible to us – until the German Battle Cruisers were plainly discernible through the mist, led by *Cardiff*.'

The heroic scale of Operation ZZ is equalled only by its pathos, for, though none could yet feel it, the war had sown the wind of change and within three decades a new generation would reap the whirlwind. In that sense ZZ was both a triumph and a tragedy, in that those who won, *and* those who lost the war, for all their valour were succeeded by politicians who could not keep the peace which, briefly, both Britain and Germany enjoyed. In token of which, Beatty, who in 1916 advocated the destruction of German industry so that the country would be forced to revert to an agricultural economy, ten years later declared in the House of Lords, 'We owe a debt of gratitude to Germany,' referring to the economic 'miracle' of her recovery.

How contrary were his feelings as the High Seas Fleet passed along his corridor of power, its armed and armoured walls four-teen miles long, the white ensigns stretching to the horizon! They were flown by nineteen subordinate Admirals in thirty-six battle-ships, eight battle cruisers and over a hundred destroyers. In all, the seventy German vessels were escorted by nearly two hundred of their adversaries.

'*Signal* 2.50 p.m.

C-in-C G.F. to Admiral von Reuter, *Friedrich der Grosse.*

The German flag is to be hauled down at 3.57 p.m. today (sunset) Thursday, and is not to be hoisted again without permission.'

The German Admiral vigourously protested at this order, as well he might, for his Government had property in those ships, a last card to play at the future Peace Conference. True, the situation was unprecedented, but whether Beatty was within his rights in making what was in effect a political decision, is still arguable. What is not open to doubt is that the signal was the primary cause of the scuttling of the interned ships in the following year. Mean-while; from Commander Ouvry's journal:—

Admiral von Reuter's protest re hauling down flag

You ordered by W.T. of 21st November p.m. that the German flag, after being hauled down at sunset, was not to be hoisted again without special permission.

On Nov 21st p.m. I urgently requested the Chief of Staff of Admiral Madden, that this order should be cancelled as the Ger-man ships have flown their flags honourably. I have not yet received an answer.

According to the terms of the Armistice, the ships were to be interned in neutral harbours or in the harbours of the Allies. As far as I know, during internment in neutral harbours during this war and former wars, flags have always remained hoisted. Had I been interned in a neutral harbour this would have been the case. Neutral harbours and harbours of the Allies are absolutely parallel according to the literal conditions of the Armistice, and to the sense of conditions of internment.

Therefore I esteem it unjustifiable and contrary to International Custom to order the striking of the War Flag of the German ships. In addition, I am of the opinion that the order to strike the flag is not in keeping with the idea of chivalry between honourable opponents.

I now therefore enter an emphatic protest against this order.

(signed) von Reuter.

Reply by Admiral Sir David Beatty

Your protest against my order regarding the flying of German colours is noted. I would draw your attention to the fact that an Armistice suspends hostilities, and that a state of war still exists between Germany and the Allies. Under the circumstances no enemy vessel can be permitted to fly the national ensign in British ports, while under custody.

(signed) David Beatty

That brisk signal would do more than the great guns had been able to do – sink the High Seas Fleet. Teutonic pride though wounded was not dead, and the insult to their flag set in train a series of events which brought about the suicide of the ships, interned in Scapa Flow after their last voyage from Rosyth. Meanwhile the spectacular triumph of the Surrender produced at home an anticlimax from which bitter controversy arose, and not only about Jutland. Beatty was accused of conducting Operation ZZ as though for his own personal gratification. If it were not so, why was the King not present with him on the bridge of the flagship? Why had Lord Fisher not been invited, for it was he who had created the Fleet; and Jellicoe, under whom the only major action had been fought?

The answers should have been obvious, but, after so long a strain, clear thinking was not in evidence. Not only senior officers, but every rating, expected, as did Lieutenant Ouvry, Assistant Gunnery Officer, that the enemy would not crawl into the cage, but fight like a trapped animal. So that was why George V came to congratulate his Navy the day *before* the event. A single well-aimed shot could have wiped out not only everyone on the bridge, but wrecked *Queen Elizabeth's* superstructure. A coordinated barrage, though suicidal, at that range would never miss. If Fisher and Jellicoe were killed like that, what would the country then think of Beatty?

No facilities existed for guaranteeing that every vessel was harmless for the Armistice terms did not allow the British to board and search. Even during the long, dreary winter at Scapa the Germans were not visited except by invitation.

So the signal was, typically, a dramatic gesture which altered neither the status of the interned ships nor the terms under which they lay. Communications were maintained with the Fatherland and no one in England knew what plots might be hatching.

Certainly Admiral Lord Fisher, that most irascible individual, took no umbrage. Nor did Jellicoe. Both men were lions of the same pride as Beatty, and it is part of natural history that lions do not deign to argue with jackals, which beset them after the kill. As for His Majesty, he had already done everything practicable to honour his Navy and their triumph. Operation ZZ was still a warlike exercise. As a Naval Officer of strictly professional competence, he would be the first to recognise that his presence might, in certain circumstances, be acutely embarrassing. Perhaps the opinion of the Navy as a whole and of the Country at large is best summed up by another old lion, Lord Beresford:—

Letter written 24th November 1918 to Sir David Beatty:—

'Your letter of 21st November is the most interesting and historical of the many in my possession, written at 6 a.m. on a day when the prestige and glory of the Grand Fleet under your command have really won the greatest sea victory in history. All our hearts go out to you and your splendid officers and men in their disappointment at there being no naval action, but a bloodless surrender is really a more brilliant achievement, illustrating the superb discipline, strength, and organisation of the forces under your command. You have added to your own renown, and the traditional glories of the British Navy, and all your old comrades of days gone by regard you with feelings of unbounded respect and affection.'

From Commander Ouvry's journal
Sunday 1st December 1918
At 12.15 the 6th B.S. (United States Battle Squadron) broke their paying-off penants and weighed anchor preparatory to leaving the Grand Fleet for their return to America. They were, however, to call at Portland for a fortnight in order to be present when President Wilson arrived in England. The ships East of the Bridge (the Forth Bridge) 'cheered ship' as the American ships passed them – *New York, Delaware, Wyoming, Arkansas, Florida* and *Nevada*. Bands played the American National Anthem, whilst the Americans rendered our National Anthem and also *Auld Lang Syne*.

Signal 12.15 p.m.

From U.S.N. New York (Flagship of Admiral Rodman)

General: The officers and men of the 6th Battle Squadron appreciate more than can be explained the never ending hospitality of the Officers and Men of the Grand Fleet. We leave with pleasant recollections of our happy stay in these waters, and with firm friendship that has grown up among us.

This signal was made to the C-in-C just as *New York* tripped her anchor.

8

RELIEF AND FRUSTRATION

To emphasise the exclusive nature of the Navy's highest rank, the establishment for Admirals of the Fleet was only three, but, because of the unprecedented circumstances, an Order in Council conferred this award on both Jellicoe and Beatty, making five such officers in recognition of their matchless contribution to the Allied victory through the attainment and maintenance of sea supremacy. In addition, Jellicoe had defeated the submarine menace which nearly starved Britain into making a separate peace; for in the worst months of 1917 out of every four merchantmen which sailed, only one returned.

They assumed their new rank on the third of April 1919, and Jellicoe remained senior not only in years, but also as First Sea Lord. Beatty however, created an historic precedent by hoisting the Union Flag at the main of *Queen Elizabeth*, signifying that he was in executive command of all His Majesty's ships. In a phrase of Churchill's this made him 'Admiralissimo'. He held this power for only four days, but it was sufficient to demonstrate that he alone, of all predecessors, contemporaries and successors, exercised a unique authority; for the rule is that on appointment as Admiral of the Fleet, either the officer is ashore, retired, or holds honorary rank; as in the case of Royalty.

On striking the Union Flag the Grand Fleet as a tactical force ceased to function, the first step in a long process of disintegration which would reduce the Royal Navy to a token force and pull down morale from its splendid summit to a state in which there would be a 'sailors' strike', almost open mutiny.

So, with Beatty beached at last, after thirty-five years during which he had seen more action than any other officer of his generation and attained unique distinction, world-wide fame, his career took on a different aspect as he moved into the rarefied atmosphere of statesmanship and world strategy. But first he gave himself six months leave.

Most of it he spent cruising in *Sheelah* with Ethel and the boys. Everywhere they went ashore he was received like royalty, and often *by* Royalty. He was particularly honoured by Albert, King of the Belgians, whose heroic defiance of the German invaders in 1914 became a vital factor in the enthusiastic popular support for England's initial war effort.

Meanwhile Jellicoe also received a special distinction in that, on the first of November 1919, he was sent on a mission to the Dominions to advise on the post-war organisation of their navies. For this purpose he virtually went back to sea, for he flew his flag, – which must also have been the 'Jack' – in the battle cruiser *New Zealand*. Subsequently, he became Governor of New Zealand, 1920, and served in that capacity for five years. Meanwhile, he had received the thanks of Parliament for his war services, and an award of £50,000. It fuelled the fires of controversy because Beatty had twice as much. On his return from New Zealand he was, belatedly, created an Earl.[1] He died ten years later, on 20th November 1935.

It was during this period that the last act in the drama of Scapa Flow was enacted, at noon on the 21st June 1919, when, before the astonished gaze of the British guardships, their prizes slowly sank.

If there had been interallied disagreements before the Surrender, which had been summarily solved, or rather shelved, by Beatty's intervention, after it they became even more marked; and at this date, only a week before the signature of the Treaty of Versailles, usually called the Peace Treaty, they were still unresolved. The main contention was between Britain and America on the one hand, France and Italy on the other, the two major Powers being unwilling to see potential rivals substantially rein-

---

[1] Previously, 1918, Viscount Jellicoe of Scapa, later Viscount Brocas of Southampton.

forced in the Mediterranean. That, however, was about the only point the United States and Great Britain did agree about, for Britain would brook no arrangement, such as a substantial addition to the American fleet, which would put her hard-won sea supremacy in jeopardy.

Unknown to any of them, for Germany was barred from all the peace discussions, their problem was being drastically solved, not by spontaneous action, as might well have occurred after those long months of confinement to their ships, but by a thorough, well coordinated plan directed by Admiral von Reuter, commanding at Scapa, and instigated, if rather obliquely, by the head of the German Admiralty, Admiral von Trotha.

When he learned that, no matter what sharing-out arrangements were made between the Allies, none of the interned vessels would return to Germany, which, he insisted, still owned them, he wrote – rather than signalled – to von Reuter, in the strongest terms. He described the internment 'in an enemy harbour' as a contravention of the armistice, perhaps recalling Beatty's signal that to hoist their flag would be a contravention. In denying the German right of ownership he described the British as 'hostile'. As Captain Stephen Roskill affirms, in his *Naval Policy Between the Wars*, this letter, dated 9th May 1919, 'amounted to an incitement to von Reuter to sink the ships; and in fact the Commander of the British Home Fleet had already warned his C-in-C that such might be the German intention.'

The Senior Officer at Scapa was then Admiral S. R. Freemantle, but the Germans waited until his battle squadron was at sea for exercises before the coded executive order was delivered by mail; 'open the sea cocks.' It is no simple matter to sink a warship from within, so skilled engineering had gone into preparing for the event, to ensure that each vessel would go down quickly and on an even keel.

With the few remaining guardships, there was little the second-in-command could do, especially when it became clear that, rather than get back aboard and try to control the inrush of the sea, crews were prepared to drown. A few destroyers were beached by the simple device of nudging them, beam on; but the bigger ships all went down and one, the most modern of the battleships, *Bayern*, settled in water not deep enough to cover her, leaving the superstructure intact.

All over the anchorage the German crews were bobbing about, some in boats, others swimming around waiting to be picked up by British whalers. In their view they had done an heroic thing. In the British view they were guilty of a string of crimes, *and* foul treachery.

Some swimmers were beaten over the head with oars, and in at least one boat those seeking rescue were fired on – not in fury by an irresponsible individual, but on the orders of an Officer.

Nor did their ordeal end there. Landed, at Kirkwall, they were reviled by the local people before being marched to a prison camp, there they were joined by von Reuter because he claimed that the operation had been planned and directed by him. The whole country was seething with indignation, without knowing why, and calling for some kind of reprisal. The Admiralty also seems to have lost its head, for lawyers were instructed to prepare charges against von Reuter. Fortunately they at least would not yield to the hysterical mood and, after due deliberation, reported that there was, in cold fact, no case at all against Reuter or his men.

And all this took place within days of the Peace Treaty's signature, after which repatriation would begin.

Still enjoying his well earned leave, David Beatty returned home in September:—

VICTORY DINNER 22nd September 1919[1]
'Portsmouth witnessed a scene on September 22nd unparalleled in the naval annals of this country. The Lower Deck of the Fleet entertained at a banquet Earl Beatty, the late Commander-in-Chief of the Grand Fleet, and a distinguished company of naval officers. The spectacle of a Commander-in-Chief sitting between a chief writer and a Petty Officer, and of other Admirals of the Fleet being guests of the lower deck was absolutely unique and unprecedented in naval records. The stirring scene at the end of the gathering, when sixteen bells were struck to show that a new era had commenced, was eloquently prophetic of the future relations between the higher and the lower branches of the Service and the Navy in General.'

[1] Portsmouth Corporation Records 1835–1927.

Though sixteen bells strike a serious note, for they are normally to be heard only at midnight on the thirty-first of December, the spirit of the occasion was by no means solemn; for the tradition of 'Good old David' was still very much alive. Since a railway strike was operating at the time it is extraordinary how many were able to get to the Guildhall on time. The Admiral himself came by car, but when he reached City Centre it was stopped by a reception committee under whose direction ropes were attached. Then a detachment of bluejackets hauled it to the foot of the steps below the imposing portico; a drill to be repeated seventeen years later, in London, when a more numerous, less cheerful escort drew, to the foot of the steps of St Paul's Cathedral, a guncarriage on which lay his coffin.

On the 1st November he took over from Jellicoe as First Sea Lord on the latter's retirement. Here too he pressed for an unusual, if not unique, distinction, to be also Chief of Naval Staff. In war the double burden would be too much for any man. In peacetime the responsibilities involved would be incompatible, so, for once, he was thwarted in his desire. And indeed the F.S.L's job at this period was at once delicate, painful, and difficult; rundown of the Fleet, and plans for international agreements which would prevent another armament race, reducing to a minimum the risk of another major war.

Christmas 1918 had been too close to the war to be merry, and David spent it quietly at Aberdour House, which Ethel had come to dislike. Indeed, she allowed her sense of proportion to become so distorted by her own frailties that when he took occasional shore leave he was hardly welcome. Christmas 1919 was very different, not only because people everywhere had recovered from the neurosis and depression which were the inevitable consequences of the long strain on short commons, but also because supplies of all kinds were getting back to normal, thanks largely to imports from America. In these altered circumstances, and the prospect of a Happy New Year, after so many which had been anything but happy, Ethel responded with one of her chameleon-like changes of temperament; eagerly leaving Aberdour to prepare Brooksby for a unique family celebration. Young David (14) came from Osborne cadet college on the Isle of Wight, Peter (9) from his preparatory school, and Little Charlie, also nine, from a similar establishment in North Wales. His mother,

Lu, was the centre of attention, for everyone knew what she had been through and wished above all things to make her feel needed, as well as appreciated.

As though to mark this watershed of war-footing to peace hopes, Pathé Gazette made a short documentary of the Admiral on the lawn in front of the house. It must have been almost the first time he had been photographed in plain clothes, and certainly with the family around him. The boys were brought in, running, to make the sequence more lively when the man turning the handle of the ciné camera felt that what he was getting on film was still the Admiral pacing back and forth, as though on quarterdeck or bridge.

As for Christmas Day, it must surely have remained in his memory, as it does, still, in mine, as one of the happiest occasions of a lifetime. It is often thought that young children have no idea of the worries and moods of grown-ups who seek to conceal their unhappiness. The Beatty boys could not know the nature of the clouds which had shadowed the past five years, but they recognised the difference made by a clear sky and the promise of sunshine. The Admiral could at last relax, and he found that playing children's games was one way of doing it. Ethel also responded. Only Lu remained somewhat aloof, in part because of her Scottish temperament, in part because she must have brooded on the last Christmas with 'old' Charlie, 1914.

Ethel had made a magnificent setting for the festival, there was an enormous tree, covered with little electric lamps, in all colours (a novelty in those days), masses of flowers and traditional decorations and a gramophone driven by an electric motor off a car's accumulator battery. Even the crackers on the luncheon table were very special, for each contained a piece of jewellery, a watch, or some other costly present. Lu had a gold ring set with a large single pearl.

Among the boys' presents two were outstanding. Young David had a scale-model boat driven by an electric motor, which we sailed in circles on the ornamental pond in front of the house. Charles had a steam locomotive, but Uncle David had forgotten it needed rails, so we had to run it without, and nearly burnt the house down when it set fire to the carpet in a corridor, being fuelled with methylated spirit which spread rapidly when the engine fell on its side.

Christmas 1919! Throughout Britain there was surely nothing like it before, and certainly not since.

As usual, Ethel's euphoria did not last long. Perhaps she thought than on relinquishing service at sea, David would at last give her all his attention. Certainly she became bored with Brooksby as she had been with Aberdour, and, after the stimulus of moving into the First Sea Lord's official residence, Mall House, annexed to the Admiralty via the famous arch, she was soon disenchanted even with that. She had always been restless. Now she resented being anywhere for long, and projected her bitterness on other people, or failing that, on external circumstances. At Mall House, for instance, she could not abide the noise from traffic, which in those days, and coming up the Mall could hardly have been much of a nuisance.

She duly moved back to Hanover Lodge, but even that, her first London home, now failed to please, and she sold it, only to try to get it back a few weeks later; for which David gave her a reprimand.

Despite the domestic turmoil he somehow managed to keep up with the work at the Admiralty, without toiling through the night, or even skipping luncheon; which says much for his Staff. It is, after all, essential for a senior officer to delegate. His duty is to appreciate a situation, decide what should be done about it, and how the plan is to be carried into effect. No one else can make such decisions, but organisation, communication, and administration properly fall on other shoulders.

And decision making was almost as arduous between 1919–1921, as it had been during the war. The Admiral had to resist a demand to become further involved in support of the White Russians, particularly to commit a naval force to the Baltic in support of Esthonian resistance to the Bolsheviks. He had to decide how the run-down of the Fleet was to be conducted, in itself a tremendous responsibility, fraught with international complications; and, as if that were not enough, he took very seriously his position in the House of Lords since it provided a forum whence his personal views would reach ears otherwise out of range.

He must have been greatly relieved when Ethel, on a characteristic impulse, set off for a restless sojourn in France in the hope that a change of scene would miraculously make her feel better;

aided by a string of fashionable doctors, including the famous Coué whose mantra was 'Every day and in every way I am better and better and better'. On her return she was indeed improved, less perhaps because of the treatments she had undergone than because she was to accompany David to the United States on a combined operation in which he would head the Naval Delegation to the Washington Conference on disarmament and at the same time represent the Government at various ceremonies to mark the war's end and the prospect of peace everlasting.

Arrived in New York, he quickly found that, instead of the dull formalities expected, he was a national hero for the United States as much as in Britain. He suffered a ticker-tape welcome, received the Freedom of the City and was presented to President Wilson at the White House in Washington. He was provided with a cavalry escort; not the decorous kind at a jog trot, but galloping alongside the car so rashly that, on coming to tram-lines, several horses fell. No man was more keen on taking calculated risks, but, contrary to popular opinion, Beatty always distinguished between boldness and rashness. While appreciating the honour, he had to convey to the Guard Commander that to risk injuring horses, let alone their riders, was unacceptable. They proceeded more carefully thereafter.

A unique Washington occasion was when, on telegraphed instructions from London, he proceeded to Arlington National Cemetery, and there, on behalf of the King, laid on the Tomb of the Unknown Warrior a Victoria Cross, 'For Valour': the only such medal not to be awarded to an individual in the British Services.

Ethel stayed on at Washinton while David continued his tour in his official capacity: Chicago, Kansas City, Philadelphia. If it seems inconsistent that Ethel did not visit her home town – where some of the Beatty charisma would have surrounded her, one has to recall that she had not been there for twenty-two years, that both her parents were long departed, and her father's peculiar Will bypassing his sons, might well have been a source of embarrassment.

An incident which in later years the Admiral used to relate with relish because it provided some light relief among all the ceremonial, occurred when he stood with Marshall Foch, Commander-in-Chief of the French armies (he used to pronounce it Fossh) at the unveiling of the Washington War Memorial. Instead of the conventional guard of honour there was a bevy of maidens, robed in white of a classical drape, each bearing a little gilt basket with the lid on. At the moment of unveiling the monument they lifted the lids and out flew a flock of doves. Still puzzled by the significance of the dress, if not of the peace-birds, Beatty made enquiries, to be told, 'But we are the Vestal Virgins, of course'.

Though he told the story with his usual gruff good humour and some embellishment, it was clear that the whole American experience made a great impression on him. Probably he had been too preoccupied with his work previously to have recognised that Britain's gratitude for American intervention was, after the war, echoed across the Atlantic by the vast majority. They recognised, if sometimes their politicians did not, that had the Allies failed, the 'American dream' was doomed.

A particularly heart-warming occasion, not unlike that dinner in Portsmouth Guildhall, was when he was entertained by those American Officers who had served under him in the Grand Fleet. Appropriately their 'club' was called Comrades of the Mist. The title could not have been more appropriate for those cold, grey northern waters, so frequently shrouded in fog.

A less agreeable event was the theft of the entire stock of wine and spirits which he had thoughtfully provided for the Delegation; knowing that although they might enjoy diplomatic immunity from the Prohibition law, it would hardly be tactful to imbibe. To avoid prying eyes, the 'cellar', instead of being in the usual commercial cases, was repacked in suitcases and trunks, then locked away. Even so it had been noted for what it really was, and, one night, bandits, ignoring the door broke through the wall at the back and lifted the lot.

Soon after the Conference began and Ethel had returned to England, in spite of genuine goodwill it became apparent that the United States had no intention of permitting British sea supremacy to continue. Consequent misunderstandings developed clashes of temperament. The Americans had not failed to read and understand how the British Empire, and indeed others, had been founded and still depended upon sea power; yet they also felt strongly that their own nascent empire needed such power no less. On their side, the British had not forgotten Wilson's Fourteen Points at the Versailles Peace Conference, and how he had threatened to walk out if his proposal for a League of Nations was not adopted. The Presidential yacht *George Washington* was ordered to raise steam preparatory to taking him home when he relented on a compromise; but that did not lessen the trend towards isolationism in revulsion at the very idea of America again being involved in a European conflict. This, when added to the insistence on U.S. naval parity with Britain, made the British delegation understandably nervous; for it might mean that if the crunch came the Royal Navy would again have to sail alone.

When America did pull out of the League, these fears were confirmed, and in this way it came about that Britain and America, having failed to preserve, for the benefit of all nations, their absolute supremacy at sea, made the Second World War inevitable. Nor did successive British Governments realise that in throwing away the peace so hardly won they were betraying both their ex-allies and their ex-enemies to the seed-bed of dictatorship, right or left. It may well have been that Hitler and Mussolini would in any case have come to power, but they would never have succeeded in their manifold aggressions had there been superior forces ranged against them from San Francisco to New York, London to Singapore, with the world's oceans and the world's air space at the pleasure of what Churchill called comprehensively The English Speaking Peoples.

The mists of 1921–1922 obscured these facts, which now seem as though they ought to have been self-evident. A secret rivalry began to develop in the demands of American and British naval experts, until in London it was seriously considered that advance strategic planning could not rule out the possibility of a clash with the United States, far-fetched though that might seem. Isolationism in the modern world is only practicable if the Power concerned is prepared to do at least some limited empire-building, which America was already doing, largely in the Pacific. That Beatty's delegates and some of their opposite numbers were no longer able to be frank, was bad enough, the former because of reservations dictated from London, the latter by political directives remote from technical matters; but when he detected signs that the Conference might fail he was glad to have to return to the Admiralty on business more urgent.

When he arrived, it was to find 'highly placed politicians were openly declaring that it was Britain's duty, in the cause of peace, to give a lead to the rest of the world by disarming still further'.[1] This would be playing straight into the hands of those in America who were determined to take over from Britannia her traditional role as ruler of the waves. Post-war limitation of Capital Ships by the Washington Conference, opened 12th November 1921.

Signatories to the Convention
   Great Britain, United States, France, Italy, Japan.

Basic Terms
   No new construction for ten years (with some exceptions)
   No battleship to exceed 35,000 tons with 16″ guns
   No cruiser to exceed 10,000 tons with 8″ guns
   Proportion of capital ship tonnage to be in accord with strategic requirements.

Strategic requirements were agreed on a scale which persisted until 1924, when the following ships were in commission:—
   USA 18, Great Britain 22, France 9, Italy 7, Japan 10.
   After which the changing political climate, new technical developments and international rivalry eroded the whole concept of 'collective security'.

'After the end of the First World War there was a virtual halt in ship construction. Naval power shifted from Britain to America and Japan. After the war the Japanese announced that they were about to build a fleet of eight battleships and eight cruisers, none of which was to undergo more than eight years service (the Conference required twenty years service before legitimate replacement). The Americans took this as a challenge and commenced a building programme of ten battleships and six cruisers'.[2] The Conference gained a respite. It could not stop the rivalry. Nevertheless solid results were achieved in that no fewer than six treaties and agreements were arrived at and included the

[1] Chalmers op. cit., p. 370.
[2] *Encyclopedia of War Machines*: Ed Daniel Bowen (Octopus) 1978.

Four Power Pact, the Treaty for the Limitation of Naval Armaments and the Limitation of Submarines and Banning of War Gases.

An essential section of the Naval Armaments Treaty was the overall tonnage permitted, and the scrapping of pre-Jutland capital ships, i.e. over 10,000 tons: Britain 20 and USA 15. Total tons permitted were:—

Great Britain	558,950
United States	525,850
France	221,170
Japan	301,320

In the deteriorating climate of international rivalry the Washington Conference was perhaps doomed from the beginning, but at least it was an attempt, indeed the first attempt, to regulate, world wide, power and possession otherwise than by gunfire. As vessels of the Great War became obsolete another effect of the Conference was their replacement by more advanced designs particularly by the Germans and the Japanese. The former's 'pocket' battleships would prove to be almost unsinkable, while the latter's most powerful units could outgun anything afloat. Perhaps the irony of the whole argument can be summed up in a single phrase: air power. Despite all the arguments about tons and guns, the navies of 1919 were already obsolete in the twenties.

Whether David Beatty had this in mind as he set about the heart breaking task of reducing to a token force the fleet which had ruled the proverbial seven seas, is a moot point, but he had certainly anticipated the growth of air power at sea, and, after the war, advocated a big aircraft building programme. Thus, as First Sea Lord his task was as onerous in its way as that of Commander in Chief, and, despite the jaunty manner he still affected, there were signs that he was losing confidence in himself and that sense of destiny he used to call *le bon Dieu*. Hitherto he did not fail because he did not believe he could fail, but now it was different. There was no tangible enemy but 'principalities and powers'; insidious, invisible and out of range. In a way it was the same with Ethel, for at last he had to accept that, whatever was really wrong with her, the doctors were as powerless to raise her dejected spirit as he was to revive the Navy.

He became increasingly dour and cynical, particularly about

politicians who interfered with his policies though they understood but little of the global strategy upon which the shrunken
Navy was based, particularly in the Far East, as for instance the
need for a major naval base at Singapore.

In so far as his changed mood affected me, I would say that what
had seemed almost sublime self-confidence became, on occasion,
bull-headed obstinacy with scant regard for other people's feelings. Outwardly our friendship – for I was no longer a boy –
remained firm, and he still behaved as though *in loco parentis*, but I
was increasingly aware that under his practiced manner lurked
something else. At first it seemed like distrust, as though he feared
I might embarrass him by making a mess of things. Only later did
I conclude that he was plagued by a guilty conscience. Even then
my admiration remained undimmed; for I could see that between
what he regarded as his failure in statesmanship and Ethel's
incurable malady, he had suffered enough stress to make anyone
bitter and twisted.

The following scrawled letter, with no punctuation, is reveal-
ing.

Thursday   Mall House
   Lu dear your letter to Tata I answer for her as she is not able to
write or read letters She has been and is very seedy and causes me
very much anxiety
I got her to Scotland and thought all wd be well in the good air and
quiet But the change did harm and she has had a nervous breakdown ever since Cannot sleep without soporifics and generally in
a terrible state of depression I am worried to death We cut short
our holiday to come and see the Doctors and they can do no good
Thank God I have work to do Much Love
                                    Yours ever
                                    David

As he quit Office in 1927, the year he was appointed to the Privy
Council, I guess the letter was written about 1924: not that it
matters, for the style is so typical of others. He preferred to write

Thursday

MALL HOUSE,
SPRING GARDENS,
S.W.

My dear your letter to Tata
I answer for her as she is
not able to write or read
letters She has been and is
Very seedy and causes me
Very much anxiety
I get her to Scotland and tho night
all wil be well in the good air
and quiet. But the change
did harm and she has had a

nervous weakdown Eur Voice i cannot sleep without Soporifics and generally in a terrible state of depression I am worried to death. We cut short our holiday to come and See the Doctor and they can do no good Thank God I have got work to do much love
Yours Ever
David

standing and had a desk made for that purpose. He preferred a very broad 'Squeezer' nib and at one time had it fitted to a goose quill, which suited the bold sweep of his lines.

Often impatient, as in the above example, his manner of speaking was equally staccato, particularly when he had no intention of listening to the other person. Of course not all his letters were like that, for in serious matters he was lucid and well balanced. Indeed, he was exceptionally competent both in correspondence and at making speeches. It was as though there were at least two contrasting sides to his personality which, as he grew older, and disenchanted, became exaggerated.

By 1924, at fifty-three, an impetuous, irascible and devious man seemed to live within the great man he had undoubtedly become. As his old friend Winston Churchill remembered him, it was always the peerless Admiral:—

Treasury Chambers
Whitehall S.W.
11th November 1924

My Dear Beatty,

I am so grateful for your kind letter of congratulations (on becoming Chancellor of the Exchequer). I am one of your great admirers, and I never cease to proclaim you as the inheritor of the grand tradition of Nelson.

How I wish I could have guided events a little better and a little longer. Jutland would have had a different ring if the plans already formed in my mind after Dogger Bank for securing you the chief command had grown to their natural fruition.

I live a good deal in those tremendous days.

Once more my sincere thanks,

Yours ever,
Winston S. C.

Tremendous days indeed! And how vast, how complex, were the forces at work in men's minds. For it now seems probable that, had Churchill's plan succeeded, the Allies might, after the destruction of the High Seas Fleet, have lost the war because America would not have come in.

During this difficult period I saw little of him, but, on being gazetted to my father's old regiment, the Sixth Foot, Royal Warwickshire Regiment, as in duty bound I went to report to him, expecting congratulations, at 17 Grosvenor Square, to which I had a key when in London. He was in the hall as I entered, standing four-square on the chequered marble floor, his back to a big, antique terrestial globe at the foot of the curving staircase. Before I could finish telling him how things were, his face contorted in one of those ferocious grimaces for which he was both famed and feared: almost a snarl.

'That's all very well Charlie, but what about Borodale?' That was a severe jolt, because I had assumed he would keep it going while I began my career and until I could afford to take over. On admitting this had been on my mind . . .

'I can't keep it on after you are of age, and it can't run itself, so you will have to send in your papers and take charge'.

'What about my career? You stopped me studying medicine, then switched me from Navy to Army'.

He simply turned away. Speechless, I let myself out into the square, eviscerated. The year was 1930, so he was still my Guardian. I had no choice but to obey.

I then appealed to the legal Trustee, a friend of my father's whom we called the Advisory. He frankly admitted that he dare not tangle with the Admiral, and who could blame him for that? So I asked what had been happening at Borodale, financially, to make Uncle take such a hard line; for as a minor I was wholly ignorant of the business side of the estate. It then appeared that, since my mother had sent most of the furniture to England for safety during the Troubles, the place had been run by the head man promoted to Steward. The result, as might have been expected, was an increasing annual loss, and, as no funds were available under my father's Will, whereby everything went to his widow, the Admiral had been meeting these losses out of his own pocket, already amounting to upwards of two thousand pounds. Even so I still had a gleam of hope, for his life-style was such that he would put the few hundred of an average year's loss on the nose of a horse. Clearly there must have been more to his sentence of banishment and a busted career than at first appeared. Let me prove that I could do better, and we would surely come to some amicable arrangement. Meanwhile, the only thing to do would be to obey orders, delay sending in my papers as long as possible, and report back when Uncle might be expected to be more amenable.

So I overstayed the long leave one gets before joining one's regiment, hoping that such a suicidal gesture might not, after all, be necessary. It was. Uncle would not relent.

Borodale was more depressing than ever before. The farm badly run and in poor heart. Such as they were, in those horse-drawn days, new machines were needed because none had been replaced since effective management ceased on my father's death. All of which required money I did not have and could not borrow, a circumstance which was quickly recognised by my employees, resulting in a furtive but evident enmity. The more I evaluated the less I liked, and this at least gave me courage to go back to Uncle David with a proposition I thought even he could not refuse; that I should break the entail and give him title to the estate out of what lawyers call 'natural affection'. This would at least keep it in the family and not make a mockery of his second title, Viscount Borodale. Then, when the economy improved, he would be able to recoup the losses.[1]

He would have none of it, though not, I think, because he wished to deprive me of my inheritance as well as my career. It is more likely that he knew no more about land that I did about sea, and could not imagine that the old adage that 'land never runs away' may be a myth. Also he may have convinced himself that, as things could hardly be worse, they must get better. It was up to me to stick it out: too soon to abandon ship. Or was he thinking of Charles, his brother? Remembering their youth, thinking this was a way to keep the old place going?

Finally, I dared to mention the money which the Advisory had told me Uncle provided to offset annual losses on the farm, for now I was 'of age', and not so naïve. For instance, I knew that for a trustee to run his ward into debt was reprehensible, if not criminal; yet the lawyer had insisted that the liability was now mine. As an act of desperation, and convinced that Uncle would be honour-bound to refuse it, I wrote him a cheque for half my

---

[1] Properly, a title 'of Borodale' could only belong to the owner thereof. When the Admiral asked Lu's permission to abrogate it, she reminded him of this yet gave her permission.

worldly wealth, four hundred and fifty pounds, expecting at least a few kind words as he tore it up; and maybe some practical gesture on his part. When we were alone one evening after dinner I passed the cheque across to him. He glanced at it, put in his pocket. It was quickly debited to my account.

Perhaps the strangest of all these incidents reflecting Uncle's ambivalent attitude, came via some of the Borodale papers I was going through. It was written to my father:—

7th Jan 1911   Brooksby Hall
                                            Leicester

Dear old Chap,

I've an old silver mug for my godson and before putting an inscription on it I want you to give me the date of his birthday and his full number of initials. I have opened an account for him at the Bank to which I will add a fiver on the 1st Jan each year so that by the time he arrives at the age of twenty-one he will have something with which to pay his Club subscriptions and help with his uniform or any expenses he will be put to at that time. It is better than giving him a footling Xmas present which would probably be of no use to him.

Whatever the annual increment, compound interest over twenty-one years would constitute a substantial windfall, and, as I knew his Bank, of course I immediately claimed it. The very least I expected was to get back those four hundred and fifty pounds. Months went by before the Bank, hardly less embarrassed than myself, admitted they could find no trace of the account. Apart from myself – and that by the most unlikely chance – only one person could have known about it. Therefore Uncle must have repossessed the balance. And he could not for a moment have imagined the letter survived, still less that I found it.

The matter became even more peculiar when the Bank traced another account of a similar nature, which had also vanished.

22nd August 1955   Lloyds Bank
'The various enquiries we have made have proved fruitless except that our ———— Branch have traced some instructions

from the late Earl Beatty which may relate to the letter you mentioned.

Our branch writes as follows:—With reference to your letter of the 17th instant and regarding a standing order given by the late Earl Beatty we give below a copy of a standing instruction dated the 5th January 1911 in favour of David Heaton Ellis.

"Please place £72:10:0 to a deposit account in the name of David Heaton Ellis and continue to place £5 to this account on the 1st January until further notice, commencing 1911, and crediting the interest to the account half yearly." We would advise you that we no longer have an account in the name of David Heaton Ellis. According to the records this order was cancelled on 14th November 1919.'

The date makes the incident bizarre, for the Admiral was then at his zenith.

It might have been interesting to trace David Heaton Ellis, but as he was unlikely to have any connection with the family – or I would at least have heard about him – it seemed no good might come if I did.

The next blow, which fell at this, my lowest ebb, was in the form of a bill from the lawyers, for costs incurred over the running of the estate, including some for the Cork property, which I had forgotten about since it seemed to produce no income.[1] Asked for details, they listed costs incurred as business management: for instance in preparation of annual accounts, for which the Advisory had to travel to Ireland. It should have been easy enough to insist that, having attained my majority I could accept no responsibility for charges incurred while in law I was still an infant; but that would have meant either a confrontation with the Admiral or perhaps a Court case. The former would, to say the least, be unproductive, for if ever there was a human 'immovable object' it was he. The latter, while leaving him unmoved, would upset other people, particularly Lu, who still regarded him as a paragon. Eventually I paid up.

---

[1] It did in fact yield, after deductions, including a mountain of mortgages, a few hundred a year; but, as the propery was not entailed, they were paid direct to Lu.

Meanwhile, in southern Ireland, things were going badly for the agricultural economy. As one old friend observed, 'The country is gone entirely to hell, and if it could it would go further.' The chief difficulty was what in official quarters was termed 'the economic war' with England over reform of the antiquated, complicated, and wholly unfair land tenure system of British origin. By witholding revenue due to England under this system, the Free State, as it then was, invited reprisals which caused a catastrophic fall in the value of farmland because Britain would accept no imports from across the Irish Sea. In Wexford this caused an accumulation of farm stock, particularly horses, while grain crops fell to such low prices, owing to a glut, that some were left standing or ploughed in. Local authorities soon felt the effects, for rates went unpaid, roads were not mended, and schools had to close because there was no money to pay the teachers.

The Borodale estate[1] had been put on the market as soon as I was legally entitled to break the entail, in October 1931, when the outlook was already bleak, but was expected to improve as the wrangle ended. Even then the Dublin Agents, Battersby & Co., valued it at a mere £18,000: not much for nearly four hundred English acres; with mansion, stud farm, various farm buildings, two lodges and four cottages. A year later they were asking £6,000, and at that figure only one offer was made, subsequently withdrawn. Even so, the Admiral was determined that I should somehow be able to keep going till better times, and, unable to believe in total disaster, as usual I conformed.

Having spent the summer taking the initial steps towards getting the farm back in good heart, living alone in the half-empty house, full of dry rot, where the only sound at night was the scurry of rats; with relief I went back to my mother's place in Wales, Trelydan Hall, near Welshpool, whence I could motor to Dingley for an occasional weekend and some hunting. The aim: to remind Uncle that he still had an inescapable responsibility for the continuity of our line, if not for the property as such, and since only eldest sons could be Beatty of Borodale the existence of the title he had misappropriated was neither here nor there; for 'of Borodale' could only mean the owner.

Even then it is unlikely that I made much impression on him,

[1] See Appendix 'D'.

but at least we did not part brass rags – naval euphemism for quarrel. Had we done so I would not have stayed on for Ethel's most lavish party. The occasion was the 'warming' of the Dingley ballroom after redecoration, the walls now painted apple green: effective if rather overwhelming, especially as hunting men were required to come 'in pink' i.e. formal evening dress of a Hunt Member; solely in order to make an agreeable contrast of colour between red and green. Others like myself, were permitted to appear in dinner-jackets, but there must have been about twenty embarrassed gentlemen; for whom this order of dress, outside the hunting season, was taboo.

None the less, the impression was all that Ethel intended, reminding me of the effect created by the Admiral in full-dress uniform, with a magnificent boat-cloak, scarlet-lined, open to show the glitter of Orders and decorations, and imperative authority symbolised by gold rings almost to the elbow. It was indeed a spectacle to grace a stage, yet the mantle fitted him, belonged to him, not as an actor but as a chief of men.

The dining room was impressive enough not to let down the ballroom décor, but it could hardly have competed with that at Reigate Priory, the ceiling of which was covered with gold leaf. This was propably not Ethel's idea but older. Either way, the effect was fantastic, since every article on the table, candlesticks, spoons and forks seemed to be of solid gold.

'Jambon', the Dingley chef, whose real name nobody seemed to know, had laid on a magnificent buffet over which he presided in his tall bonnet, assisted by two other cooks. Footmen in knee breeches and buckled shoes served Champagne of 1911 vintage – Möet or Mumm – still at its best. After a while, pleasantly awash, the company's conversation, hitherto subdued, became louder; and Ethel led us back into the ballroom where decorous entertainment had been arranged, so that beautiful women and brave men would be quiet and still while she appreciated the picture they made.

The 'entertainer' proved to be one of the great violinists of the day, who naturally supposed he had been engaged for a serious concert and accordingly rendered one or two distinctly highbrow pieces. When the hunting field recovered from their surprise there was remarkably little applause, and one bold thruster asked for something more to their taste. It could have been John Peel or the

Posthorn Gallop. Though coldly polite, the maestro made it plain that he had no intention of obliging – even supposing he knew what they were talking about – and the party therefore relapsed into hubbub, leaving him severely alone. He was so obviously out of his element, and deeply hurt, that I went over to him, and despite being as much out of his element as he was out of ours, made what conversation I could. Perhaps we both made rather too much of appearing to be interested in one another.

After a while a band appeared. The maestro and his accompanist left with dignity but in dudgeon, and everyone became as hearty as could be, though few were versed in the current vogue for dancing cheek to cheek. Suddenly there was a heavy thud as someone crashed to the polished floor. Those near him stopped in their tracks. I noticed he was strangely sprawled, with one leg twisted under him. And it was Young David.

The band stopped. Uncle shoved his way through the crowd to bend over his heir. Someone suggested sending for a doctor but the Admiral brushed that aside. Within a few seconds the casualty was on his back with two men taking orders. One got him under the arms the other grabbed the uninjured leg. One hand on the other knee, and its fellow on the ankle, Uncle made a quick tug, then ran his hands over the limb as I had often seen him do with a horse.

'Dislocated', he said, 'I think it has gone back in. If so, we've been lucky. The longer a joint stays out the harder it is to get back'. With that he helped Young D to his feet, who after waggling the leg and then gingerly letting it take his weight, returned to his partner.

The party broke up in the small hours. I had not been in bed more than a few minutes when there was a knock at the door and the resident nurse, of delectable appearance and considerable charm, entered. She was still in uniform and carried a wine glass brimming with something brown.

'Lady Beatty noticed you were looking rather peaky', she said, 'and thought a little nightcap would do you good'.

'What is it, brandy?'

Nurse smiled cryptically. 'What else?'

'Very kind of Aunty. Give her my best thanks. And just put it down there' (indicating bedside table). 'Good brandy should be slowly sipped.'

'Lady Beatty particularly asked that I should see you drink it up and bring back the empty glass. She really seemed quite worried about you.'

'Oh, very well then. It calls for no great effort on my part. And thank you for bringing it. When you came in I was somewhat taken aback.'

So she handed me the brandy and I drank it down, speculating about that Mona Lisa smile.

'Prime old cognac,' I announced, handing her the empty glass.

Before first light I had already been to the bathroom several times, and had to conclude that the spirit had been spiked with an aperient, the taste of which had not come through because I had gulped it down. So that was the reason for the enigmatic smile! Then what on earth put the idea into Ethel's head? In one of her manic moods she was apt to turn on someone for no apparent reason; but why me? Later, I discovered it was more than that. She had disapproved of me making friends with the maestro when everyone else was giving him the cold shoulder, and this was her idea of a suitable punishment. No doubt her revenge would be complete when she discovered, through the nurse, what effect the purge had had. So I resolved not to reveal anything to anyone. The effect would soon pass, or ought to, unless she had tried to poison me; and I hardly thought her capable of that; nor would the nurse have been her accomplice. Slowly I began to feel better, and by breakfast time was able to carry on as though nothing untoward had happened during the night. There was a temptation to make a funny story of it, but the laugh could easily go against me. No, the thing to do was to get into the car and, having found an adequate excuse, be clear of the house – particularly the nurse – before Ethel came down and started asking solicitous questions about my health.

Not until that autumn, when I was invited to Grantully Castle, near Aberfeldy in Perthshire, could I be sure that the incident had been forgotten, or at least forgiven; and it was so. As the peak of the grouse season was long past, the house-party was almost entirely family, and I left at the end of a week with the feeling that, after all, to them I still belonged. This was in contrast to the scale of the sporting rights which the Admiral leased from the owners, as indicated by the following extract from the *Daily Telegraph* of 8th January '79:—

'In January 1979 the estate and Castle of Grantully, amounting to 8,750 acres were sold for two million pounds. The castle dates from about 1400. The vendor was the 23rd Stewart of Grantully. The buyer was the Rothesay Investment Trust "as a commercial venture".'

My grouse shooting had been limited to the moors of North Wales, so I was happy not to have been bidden to the big days when anyone's reputation depends upon his individual contribution to the bag; which in the case of Grantully ran high: several thousand in the short season. It was more agreeable when Uncle and I walked together 'on the hill' looking for pot-luck. He was a good companion then, and a fair shot; though, typically, he was out to kill; and damn silly conventions such as it being 'unsporting' to shoot save on the wing. On hand and knees he would stalk a brace of partridge, and knock them off, right and left before they even knew he was there.

Out hunting in the Shires he also asserted an individual style. Though he had put on weight, and, with his thickset look seemed unlikely to be a flyer, the combination of superb hunters, first-rate horse-manship and an intimate knowledge of the country, justified him in taking an individual line whenever practicable. Conversely, he had no patience with any member of the field who appeared to be out for exercise rather than determined to be in at the breaking-up of the fox. At the other extreme was the Prince of Wales, whose keenness was out of proportion to his ability. Our Admiral admired the former, but so much deplored the latter that, after the Prince had come a cropper trying to follow him, he may well have had something to do with the King's decision to stop 'Edward P.' (as he used to sign) steeple-chasing; though he did go on hunting. As to the Admiral's style, here is part of a letter from Sir Gerald Glover of Pytchley House:—

'He infuriated me by always arriving at the Meet with beautiful horses and followers known as "second horses". He went brilliantly and all his bloodstock were of the highest quality and would jump anything instantly from stand-still. He had, however, one most unattractive habit in that as soon as we landed up beside a fox covert and waited to let the hounds in he would pull out of his pink coat a cigar of a particularly nasty variety and light it, making the air intolerable for his neighbours. I often remonstrated with him over this to which he had a blind ear, not eye, and we never cured him of his cigars to the last day of his hunting. It must have been a tremendous strain on his lungs and bad for his horses, but he would do it!'

The Admiral was by no means an addict, of tobacco or anything else. He would not allow himself to become dependent upon anything or anyone, but he did fully appreciate the good things of life. As for his physical stamina, it became clear that he was no longer quite so tough after two bad falls. The first broke his arm, and as soon as the bone knit he mounted the same Irish maverick to teach it a lesson, and was again heavily thrown. This time his jaw was so badly broken that for months it was wired up. He could speak only out of the corner of his mouth, and had difficulty in swallowing anything but liquids; a restriction which probably irked him less than it would some people, for, as Sir Gerald observes, 'It seemed that he liked a little brandy to reinforce his natural spirit'.

Of course; and so did they all, in moderation; for to those hard-riding characters stamina was a first consideration, though not of the same kind as that needed by athletes. They deserved what Churchill neatly terms 'medical comforts' to maintain their demanding way of life; and when it could no longer continue they tended rapidly to decline. When the Admiral regained the use of his jaw he had to make some concessions to advancing years. Yet in those months of disability he must have done some deep thinking, with the result that from my point of view he became more considerate; though the notorious facial tic was worse than ever. Perhaps for the first time he came to realise what a mess he had made of my life, and that, far from it being my fault that Borodale was on the rocks, he could have either prevented the wreck or towed it clear, with little loss to himself; and, in view of the title, the prospect of at least a moral gain.

Even so, he still did not offer to organise a salvage operation to save what we still could; but, through most of the four years from his retirement in 1927 until Ethel's death four years later, he made it plain that I was *persona-grata*. This suited me admirably, in particular the weekend house-parties at Reigate Priory; for he relished the company of young people. It was said that on one occasion he invited, in Ethel's absence, the entire Gaiety Chorus;

but of this, confirmation is lacking. It could have happened. I well remember the wry grimace he made when he came into the hall to find in my arms the bride of the Chilean Ambassador, but newly appointed to the Court of St James. That she had in fact slipped on the polished floor, with its even more slippery rugs, was something which, though perfectly true, he did not seem to believe.

It is a magnificent house, rich in historical associations which demand respectful treatment, though whether the piper whom Ethel brought from Scotland comes into that category is doubtful. In full Highland dress he paraded precisely at eight o'clock every morning, marching the long length of the face of the house, pipes at full blast. A skirl over the hill, on the march or at a graveside, moves many a sassenach to tears of wonder and amaze, but not at Reigate, Surrey, as a meaningless routine. The Priory is supposed to be haunted – or was. As a form of exorcism the piper was probably as efficacious as bell, book and candle.

Ethel also responded to this lighter mood. It was almost like the silver lining effect of the fabulous 1919 Christmas when the war-clouds parted. She had lately acquired one of the first electric gramophones, called a Panotrope. Disguised as a piece of antique furniture, it stood by the newel post at the bottom of the grand staircase in the Priory's biggest room. The place had a long association with royalty, which continued till Edward VII stayed there, and also with the Navy; for, 'A meeting had been set up at Reigate Priory. Churchill and most of the Cabinet were present. The old Admiral (Fisher) faced them like the wise old man before his appelants.'[1] Hardly the place for raucous music, but the machine had a huge output, frequently rocked the dignified shades with 'jazz' and seemed somehow to upset Ethel. Perhaps it reminded her of youth, in the past tense. Even so, instead of giving way to menopausal depression she was determined to take a new lease on life and looks. Nor was it only artifice which made her seem younger and better looking; for she had always kept her figure, and her basic features, never flabby, retained their original symmetry. To show how much better she felt, I was shown how she set about acquiring the latest fashions.

---

[1] November 1914 on his return as First Sea Lord following the resignation of Prince Louis of Battenberg. (Hough (R): *First Sea Lord* (Fisher) p. 512.

Before each season came round *le grand coutourier*, Worth, designed for her whatever garment she specified for morning, noon, or night. Transferring his ideas to fabric, pinned on a mannequin of her build and colouring, they were then sketched, hand-coloured and bound in an elegant folder. The one she showed me at Reigate contained perhaps twenty plates in water-colour which in these days would probably be regarded as serious art. Having brooded on the plates, all she had to do was note the 'numbers' she approved, along with any changes which took her fancy, and perhaps this was the origin of the enduring habit of referring to Paris originals as 'numbers' such as 'the little black number'.

Her life-style though then usual among the very rich, in retrospect seems fantastic, partly because of the scale of her living and partly because, except health, it seemed that everything desirable could be bought, regardless of cost. To some extent David shared and enjoyed conspicuous wealth, for which reason he was sometimes uncharitably referred to as 'the Nightclub Admiral'; and he certainly enjoyed the lighter side of life to an uncommon extent, considering that, after a most arduous passage through perilous seas, he was nearly sixty. Nor did he ever permit himself to show the sorrows which he continued to bear with characteristic fortitude.

If the 'unmanning' of the Royal Navy had been a heartbreaking task, it was no less depressing to recognise increasing signs of social upheaval both in Europe and the United States. The very strata of society upon which Society and Empire equally depended for stability were cracking up, and, apart from the extremists of both right and left, there seemed to be no prospect of re-establishing the traditional values for which the Great War had been fought. No wonder he enjoyed every diversion within his long reach, from cabaret to music in St Paul's; and he continued to do everything in style, not, as frequently alleged, out of conceit, but because he really was *homo superior* and behaved as such. His dark green Rolls-Royce, for example, did not carry the famous mascot 'spirit of ecstasy' but the old Beatty crest[1] in massive silver. When he took people to a cinema the Manager would be waiting in the foyer, and at least on one occasion when I was there, the film was delayed until we were seated.

[1] See Appendix 'C'.

In contrast there was his racing style. At Epsom for instance, his car was at once welcomed and a channel through the crowd swept for it. Everyone recognised him, and he knew everyone who was anyone. In the spacious box, close to the winning post, there was a telephone next to the buffet table with a few bottles of Champagne and other sophisticated comforts. When he came back from the paddock with a marked card he could get straight through to his bookmaker, and might wager anything up to a monkey, £500, on a single race. Whether he won or lost made not the slightest difference to his demeanour. This characteristic had been acquired the hard way, for at sea it had been essential that he appear neither elated by success nor depressed by failure: an almost Oriental inscrutability in sharp contrast to the showmanship he sometimes affected. And behind it all was the colossal background of his authority.

On 1st July 1925 he wrote to Ethel at Nice:—

'I dined with the Admirals and Captains of the Grand Fleet last night (in London), a very representative gathering of over 140 officers, many old friends made enquiries after you, and many I had not seen since the old war days. Of course the greater number of them were retired, but still there were at least 75 Admirals present, and on the whole it was a great success. Jellicoe and I were the guests of the evening and we were like brothers . . . I am just off to a meeting on the Security Pact with France, Germany and Belgium, and there is further trouble over Morocco and the Tangier Zone.'

This is one of a long series of letters spanning the six years 1921–1927 when Ethel was almost continuously abroad, in all, thirty-one months. She had acquired a villa at Biarritz but, as usual, wandered freely. Among the places where she remained long enough to receive letters were: Aix-les-Bains, Hyères, Cap Ferrat, Baden-Baden, Nice, and Freiburg. At this last she stayed at Dr Martin's sanatorium while at Baden-Baden it was at Dr Dengler's establishment. Out of this extraordinary pattern, considering how much David needed her in his exalted rôle, social as well as Service, emerges another factor in addition to her ill-health: that the marriage was again under great strain Except in the light of previous crises, to be travelling abroad for roughly one month in three is otherwise inexplicable. Not only did she live like a woman detached, in so far as they still needed it, the boys, aged twelve and seventeen were left in his care; and so were those elaborate domestic establishments in town and country.

He must often have been grateful that his responsibilities, heavy enough to have brought most men to their knees, prevented him from following her into melancholia. Instead, she was ever in his heart, and mind. And it must have occured to him, even obsessed him, that, for lack of a cure, she might feel there were only two courses open to her: desert him or become a long-stay patient, or both. Was that the real reason she 'went into retreat'? Is that why he drove himself to write the cascade of letters, all intended to strengthen family ties, strained almost to breaking point? Against her case history of twenty years the answer can hardly be anything but affirmative.

9

AFTERMATH

At last realising how disastrous had been the course he set for me since my father's death when he became my guardian, the Admiral gave me to understand that I would still be able to embark on an alternative career; with at least his moral support. Neither of us mentioned how he had prevented me studying medicine, switched me from Navy to Army, then deprived me of a Regular Commission at a time when there was no future for the Irish estates and I had no qualifications for industry or commerce. We both knew the circumstances: too well.

He still believed that Borodale was worth enough to give me a new start, and issued his orders accordingly. As usual I had to obey, though resolved not to spend more time over there than absolutely necessary. For his prestige was now such that, with him behind me, many doors would open at my knock. There were no such doors in rural Ireland, and, although not yet 'of age' I had no illusions about that country's derelict economy. If Borodale could be sold at all, it would not produce enough capital on which to build.

As a result of our rapprochement we saw more of each other at this period, 1927–1932 than at any other since he played 'bears' with us boys at the glorious Christmas of 1919. Nearly every weekend, when in England, I was welcome to Ethel's houseparties, and if they included fewer of his brother officers than one might expect, it was after all natural for her to prefer more fashionable company, especially with titles. Even so I came to know some of his contemporaries quite well, and was aware that, they, like the Admiral himself, were extremely worried.

The bitter fruits of the Washington Conference were everywhere evident, particularly in the corridors of power. The international order was rapidly falling to pieces and at the same time Britain had lost sea supremacy under conditions which made it impossible to regain in the forseeable future.[1] What remained of the Navy was starved of material, of low morale, restive about pay and conditions; reflecting the way in which the economic infrastructure of the West was cracking up, particularly in the United States. It would reach the nadir of dissolution on Black Monday, 24th October 1929, when irresponsible speculation on Wall Street became sheer panic, not only among financiers but by every section of the public. In less than a month thirty thousand million dollars were lost in stock values, and the average price of securities was more than halved. This must have had a serious effect on Ethel's income, though on the surface there was no indication that she and David were cutting back: except that she sold the yacht.

Politically, Britain was unstable as never before in time of peace. Elected in January 1924, Labour's first prime minister Ramsay Macdonald, was forced in October to form a National Government, in which, however the old guard with whom the country had weathered such terrific storms, was hardly represented. Not even Churchill was in office.

Unrest was steadily growing, unemployment rising. Even the Dole had been cut, resulting in 'hunger marches'. The going rate was eighteen shillings a week for a man, five for his wife and two for each child, barely enough to keep body and soul together. In 1926 came the General Strike, which fizzled out because it only made matters worse for the workers. By the end of 1930 there were two and a half million unemployed while outside their patient ranks every kind of extremism flourished, as it did on the Continent. Political factions proliferated, and, Red, or Black – for Anarchy – they flourished in blood-contaminated soil.

So there again was that writing on the wall. Not only had the Allies lost the peace and beggared, in Britain, the country which was to have been 'a land fit for heroes to live in'. Moderates and extremists alike, though as yet they knew it not, were hell-bent for another war: as powerless to stop and think as lemmings

---

[1] 'History shows no instance of sea supremacy once yielded being regained.' Earl Beatty speaking as Lord Rector of Edinburgh University in his inaugural address, 28th October 1920.

hastening to the brink of their destruction. And this time the odds would be against us from the start, for neither the will nor the wealth of 1914 were any longer there, and, as the Admiral knew better than most, having repudiated her commitments in Europe, particularly the League of Nations, and naval solidarity with Britain in the event of war, America was certain to stand aloof: as indeed happened – until Pearl Harbor.

Not that the United States lacked problems of their own. A case could indeed be made for isolationism, but such considerations were remote from the Admiral. All that mattered to him in the personal equation was that he had been let down by his in-laws, our cousins, whose special relationship should, in his judgement, have become a permanent marriage between the English-speaking Peoples. There was therefore no time for explanations nor excuses, for any sort of compromise was anathema to him. He would not have paused to reflect that Americans had every reason to mind their own business and let the war-minded nations mind theirs. Unlike the English Channel, the wide Atlantic was still a formidable barrier, a moat big enough to guarantee security from invasion so long as the US Navy and Air Force maintained command of it, if need be unaided. To them the alliance which won the war had done its work when the Covenant of the League of Nations came into being after the Treaty of Versailles in 1920. That America subsequently pulled out of the seething European pot was in no sense a betrayal. It merely recognised, as every schoolboy knew, that, despite idealists like Woodrow Wilson, history is a narrative of conflict, occasionally interrupted, as in a boxing match, by intervals for recovery which it were absurd to call peace because the bell must soon go for the next round.

Such were the ominous circumstances when the Admiral stood down as First Sea Lord, in 1927. He had done more than any other man to embody the spirit later dramatised by Nöel Coward under the title *In Which We Serve*. Not only with guns but also with words he fought for the traditional concept of patriotism as the pre-eminent virtue: *dulce et decorum est pro patria mori*. This was not nationalism, nor racism, but an ideal upon which, with all its shortcomings, Pax Britannica was based. Not even a Vote of Thanks by both Houses of Parliament, an Earldom, the Order of Merit, and a hundred thousand pounds, could counter a sense of bitter disappointment with the sweet taste of fulfilment. Nightclub Admiral indeed! Even if such mockery had a germ of truth in it – which indeed it had, against what he had achieved how small a thing, and how innocent?

If it were trivial in relation to the past, it was minuscule in relation to the present:—

'The supply of the essential ingredient for the working of our civilisation – money, had started drying up after the October 1929 collapse of the stock market. Wages were cut for those with jobs. Part-time work was the rule everywhere. The whole country was spiralling down into unimaginable chaos. Oil in East Texas stayed in the ground because there was little demand for gasoline at any price . . . It was not too far-fetched to foresee the extinction of the entire middle class unless something like a miracle was achieved in a hurry.'[1]

Something like a miracle did happen in America, and was duly noted in Russia *as such*, but this increased the case for pulling out of world commitments. Franklin Roosevelt to Colonel House in September 1935, after Hitler had come to power:—

'They (the isolationists) imagine that if the civilisation of Europe is about to destroy itself through internal strife, it might just as well go ahead and do that, and that the United States can stand idly by.'[2]

So much for the ominous horizon to the West when there broke over the Admiral's head the scandal which became known as 'The Harper Report', based on the allegation that he had abused his position at the Admiralty by distorting an official account of the Jutland affair. Even in 1980 the issue is still emotive in some circles, but the details of the sordid tale are really no longer relevant except as an indication of how blind and bitter was the resentment between pro-Beatty and pro-Jellicoe factions. It has to be recognised now, though it must have seemed very odd then, that our Admiral was perfectly capable of breaking the rules. That he should do so for petty gain is improbable in the extreme, but if he believed that he alone could set the record straight then, even against the evidence, he would surely do so. He was, after all, accustomed to *making* the rules.

---

[1] Roosevelt (E) and Brough (J): *The Roosevelts of the White House.*
[2] ibid. Letter written September 1935.

There were two principal accusations, both, to a landsman, of trivial import. He is alleged to have 'divided his fleet' and so deprived the battle cruisers of the powerful support of the fifth battle squadron at a critical time, after the initial clash with Hipper's force, from which he emerged so badly mauled. What happened was that in making an alteration of course the slower ships fell astern, and never caught up as the battle cruisers hurried to conform to Jellicoe's plan. Further it is alleged that the turn itself was a mistake, not by intention but as seamanship. Some writers maintain it was a complete circle, others an 'S' turn. The accusation is that Beatty himself altered the record, or caused it to be altered, from the former to the latter, because of the implication that he had lost 'seven valuable minutes' by the manoeuvre. Few printed accounts admit that both versions have truth in them. As the turn commenced it was intended to be 180°. When *Lion* went on turning, and not till then, was it noticed there was a fault in the gyro compass.[1] Corrected, the course did produce a peculiar track, as it must have done, from nearly full circle back to the originally intended bearing.

The trouble over the record started in 1919 and never died down in the Admiral's lifetime. It is a complex story, and of little interest save to naval historians, except in that it impugns the Admiral's character. Whether or not he had something to hide is now an academic question, but if he had, it must have been relatively trivial. Here are some of the more important facts behind the wrangle.

In his original despatch of the battle, Beatty, on 17th July 1916, 'corrected' the turn to an 'S', and signed it. Later, track charts, logs of ships other than *Lion*, and eyewitnesses, affirmed that the original (circle) version was correct, and that it occurred at a critical point of the battle, 6.45 p.m. In 1919, the Harper Report, commissioned by the Admiralty at the request of Parliament while Beatty was still afloat, reopened the matter and concurred with his critics, after having access to all the records. Then First Sea Lord, Beatty read it before it could be issued and promptly suppressed the whole thing, for a reason which to him must have been good enough to justify such drastic action. At this Captain

---

[1] Such a compass was fitted with an alarm bell to ring if a fault developed. In this instance the alarm did not sound.

Harper vehemently protested, and he is described as 'six foot two of robust New Zealand integrity.' As a result, a note was attached, or it was agreed that it should be attached, giving reasons for the amendment. Whether that was done or no, the Report never reached the House of Commons, which had called for it in the first place to allay the controversy.

'In its place, a year later, 1920, the Jutland Despatches containing simply the original reports made by commanding officers after the battle with all their claims of gunnery and torpedo successes, made in good faith but greatly exaggerated, particularly in the battle cruisers and destroyers, were published. A mass of technicalities, it was largely unintelligible to the man in the street and the newspaper correspondents.

In vain, Jellicoe, Wemyss and Admiral Sir Francis Bridgeman, another former First Sea Lord, appealed for the Harper Report to be published. Nothing less would remove the smears that had accumulated over the years on Jellicoe's name or reduce to reasonable proportions the ludicrous adulation that always accompanied the mention of Beatty.

Instead, in 1924, a volume entitled *Narrative of the Battle of Jutland* appeared. The contentment of Jellicoe's declining years can hardly have been sweetened by the fact that, though in an appendix he was permitted to counter some of the statements made in this book, the Admiralty, the body which he had served faithfully for so long and finally headed, included footnotes to Jellicoe's remarks refuting his contentions . . . It was not until 1939 that Corbett's *Naval Operations* vol iii, was revised to include the German signals intercepted by the Admiralty during the night of May 31st/June 1st, and never passed to the Commander-in-Chief at sea.'[1]

The Harper Report was eventually published, in the late sixties, under the auspices of the Naval Records Society of which Captain Roskill happened, at that time, to be Vice-Chairman, when the second Earl, 'Young' David, had authorised him to do what, hopefully, would become the Definitive Life. He was already deep into his subject when Young David heard of this matter and, 'It was a source of real sorrow to me that the second Earl chose to pick a quarrel with me because the Navy Records Society pub-

[1] Macintyre (D): *Jutland*.

lished 'the Harper Papers' about Jutland. In fact the decision to do so was taken by the Council as a whole . . . This quarrel of course made the biography hopeless – especially as I knew David 2nd Earl had suppressed the draft biography by Shane Leslie because it told about his father's disastrous marriage and hinted at his love affairs.'[1]

So there it all is, or nearly all, and what remains hidden can now be of little consequence. No smoke without fire? Another question is implicit. If power corrupts, does not personal integrity, carried to excess, give to a man who honestly believes in, 'my country, right or wrong' a conviction, even against reason, that the same aphorism applies to himself?

Outside the feuding factions their wrangle meant little or nothing. Beatty's position was, in the popular mind, unassailable, and his reputation as a national hero continued to grow. His speeches, particularly in the House of Lords, were widely reported, and membership of His Majesty's Privy Council gave him an aura which was hardly justified by the diminished role of that august body. Though it dates from Norman times the Council has had no executive function since the reign of Queen Anne:—

'From the accession of George I the Privy Council may be described as a purely formal body meeting on purely formal occasions to transact purely formal business'. Though in the thirties the Council was rather more exclusive the trend is illustrated by the fact that by the sixties there were more than three hundred 'right honourable Lords and others of Her Majesty's Most Honourable Privy Council.' It is a peculiarity of membership that it lasts only during the reign of the Monarch who conferred the honour, though his or her successor may deem a particular member worthy of re-appointment. In the case of Beatty therefore his membership would have ceased with the death of George V and as his own death occurred shortly afterwards there would have been no time to make a new appointment.

By this time Ethel was suffering from a progressive deterioration of the blood vessels, though she herself would not have been told lest the knowledge that she might suffer a stroke increase her

---

[1] Private communication from Captain Roskill 22nd January 1979.

chronic anxiety. On 17th July 1931 she died, suddenly, at Dingley, of cerebral thrombosis (blood clot on the brain). The 'witness at the death' was Effie Campbell, probably a nurse, whose address is given as 'Ebost, Dunvegan, Skye.'

As always when someone who has long been in close companionship abruptly excarnates, an immediate effect is a visual flashback . . . Every Sunday morning after church, at which the Admiral read the lessons as though to his own ship's company, his guests, instead of going back to the house a few hundred yards further on, used to follow Ethel to the stables. At the gates of the yard stood the head lad, wearing a hard hat, white stock, breeches and leggings; in his hand a trug full of carrots, washed and split lengthwise.

Along the line of loose-boxes, their half-doors open, appeared a dozen alert heads and glossy necks. The horses immediately recognised her, and whickered with pleasure as she went from one to another, offering on the palm of her narrow hand two halves of a carrot each. That she had a way with horses was well known in the Shires, and if she did not possess the fabled 'horseman's word', she certainly had an almost magical touch with some of them.

Tagging along behind, came a straggle of guests, some of whom would be taken by the Admiral into the commodious boxes, meticulously clean and with long straw deep on the floor. They would be asked their opinion of each animal: no easy task since all were superb, particularly the weight-carriers, which looked, despite the evidence of *pur sang*, as though they could carry a knight in armour. Few people dared to make any serious criticism.

Thus Ethel at her best remains in memory's sieve, while trivia and misshapen thoughts fall through the mesh and are forgotten.

Though as plain fact her transition was a merciful release, not only for herself, David took it hard:—

Grantully Castle 18th Aug 1932

'I cannot get used to the altered circumstances. We are strange creatures and truly Conservative, and I miss poor little Ethel far more than I can say, forget all the difficulties and remember only the sweetness of her, and try and console myself with the thought that she is happy and at peace, and her turbulent soul is at rest. Time alone can help, or at least I hope so, and I have to keep a stiff lip to help the Boys along. They miss her terribly. She did so much for them. It all seems terribly strange at present. Every corner reminds one. It is hard to sever a link of 30 years of a very stormy life. We shall go on living at Dingley, and I want to sell Brooksby, and for the present lease the Priory.[1]

Indeed, despite stresses which would have broken most marriages, they always preserved an effective unity, dissolved by her departure, leaving him as it were halved. It must have been more than the honour code which kept him true to her. Were it not so, she would not have been able to hurt him so often and so much; whether out of jealousy, spite, or because she could not help it. If 'each man kills the thing he loves', then every woman yearns to be loved to death. The signs are often conspicuous in terms of provocation, and the more hateful she is the more love she demands. Except when out of control, this need not be either wrong or crazy, for it is normal to discover that to love the lovable is not enough and much too easy. To go on loving the soul of someone who often appears anything but lovable is something else; and this surely defines the paradox of their mutual fascination. Each in the other saw something transcendental, and though she was so often tiresome, he saw through her tantrums.

Her envelope was buried beside the path leading from the Hall to the door of Dingley Church. The horizontal slab is inscribed, 'A good friend to sailors during the Great War and after.' Fair comment, for her benevolent interest in bluejackets was by no means confined to Christmas turkeys (one for each Mess), and the conversion of the yacht *Sheelah* to be a floating hospital. Brooksby had been a convalescent hospital during the war. Of faith she had little, either in gods or men. Of hope, latterly, she had none, but in charity she could be admirable; and is so remembered.

Having at last reached an inescapable dead-end, I closed the heavy

[1] Letter to the Duchess of Rutland.

front door of Borodale behind me for the last time; taking the knocker with me. For a time my step-grandmother 'Mouse' and her son Henry, who was always known as 'Pat', were going to run the place as a guest-house for sporting visitors to Ireland. But this did not come to anything and eventually Mouse and Pat were forced to the conclusion that nothing remained but to pull the mansion down. It is true that Mouse could have appealed to the Admiral before taking this final step, but she was too proud to do so.

There was also the outstanding matter of the sale of contents and effects which Mouse did not want, and, when no cheque appeared, a protest to the auctioneer brought only a pathetic note to the effect that he had been 'caught in the gloom' i.e. gone bankrupt. It was hard to think kindly of Uncle David, who had urged me not to abandon ship, and when it sank beneath me, appeared to regard the incident as closed. What makes his apparently callous attitude the more extraordinary, and ambivalent, is that he produced for my coming-of-age an expensive if rather useless present from Asprey: a fitted dressing-case.

The whole sequence by which he abandoned Borodale was, at the time, as improbable as it was painful. Perhaps, having become accustomed over the years with Ethel, to live with money galore, he could not now grasp how true is the anxiom, for most people, that money is not 'the root of all evil.' The lack of it is. Or perhaps, as with others of great wealth, after the slump had cut into dividends, he really felt he must be hard up; despite the fact that an Admiral of the Fleet never goes on pension or even half-pay. Technically, he is still available for Service if required. Then of course there was the £100,000 voted by Parliament, and there was no inflation.

At this period Peter was my mooring: safe, loyal, dependable. Despite increasing disability he not only revived my shaken morale but, my early novels having failed, backed a Company of Adventurers in which I became a Director, Safari (Africa) Ltd of 3 St James' Square. It would have been a good success had it not been for Mussolini's war with Abyssinia which stopped our clients from venturing through the Mediterranean on the way to Mombassa and our base in Tanganyika. The Company folded, voluntarily. I found another job. In Ireland the House of Beatty was reduced to rubble:—

TEN SHILLINGS FOR BORODALE!
MANSION AND 146 ACRES SOLD FOR TEN SHILLINGS
Deal by Out of Work Labourer

'That Borodale House (County Wexford), the ancestral home of Earl Beatty, and an estate of 140 acres was bought by an unemployed labourer for 10/-, was revealed at Enniscorthy District Court yesterday.

The man, John Murphy of Mary Street, Wexford, was prosecuted by the Free State Department of Agriculture for unlawfully felling 214 trees without permission from the Department.

In cross-examination by Mr Kelly, State Solicitor, Murphy said he was an unemployed labourer under medical treatment and that he bought the house from the estate of the late Flight Lieutenant Henry Longfield Beatty on September 12, 1934.

He appointed a man called Culleton as his agent and gave him permission to sell firewood. The agent sold the trees and took full responsibility for it. The price paid for Borodale and the lands was ten shillings.

Mr F. M. O'Connor, solicitor for Murphy, said that the late Flight Lieutenant Beatty made several attempts to sell Borodale as, owing the heavy rent (*head-rent*, a peculiar Irish institution) of about £300 a year, he was unable to keep it.[1] He then sold it to Murphy who was not in a position to look after it.

The District Justice said Murphy was liable to a fine of £1,070. He took into consideration all the circumstances and imposed a fine of, roughly, 2s 6d per tree, totalling £25.'

The paper does not reveal – and why should it – that F. M. O'Connor was also the lawyer who acted for me in drawing up the Conveyance for Mouse; so the chances are that, acting for her, it was he who produced a ten shilling note for the unfortunate Murphy.

When I first read that clipping, I had no idea that Pat was dead. In fact he had been killed, and in circumstances so bizarre that I have always felt he may have been the last of us to be affected by

---

[1] Quoted from undated press cuttings, probably *Daily Mail* or *Daily Express* in the author's collection. See also Appendix 'D'.

the mysterious influence I call the 'bane'. Here is another newspaper excerpt:—

'AIRCRAFT CLOCK STOPPED AT 9.15

A column of smoke was seen pouring from R.A.F. Flying Boat K3595 before it crashed in flames in the mountains near Messina, 15th February 1935.

The bodies of the nine members of the crew were placed in five coffins and carried on the shoulders of peasants to the little church in the village of San Fillipo. Later they were taken to the naval hospital at Messina to await the arrival of the British cruiser *Durban*, which will transport them to Malta . . . The machine was one of the four Royal Air Force flying boats which left Britain in January for an 8,000 mile flight to Singapore. Two of them on their way from Naples to Malta ran into thick fog over Sicily nearing the Straights of Messina. One succeeded by "blind" flying in reaching Malta. The K3595, however, apparently lost direction and crashed in flames into the side of a mountain five miles from San Fillipo at a height of about 2,250 feet.'

Naples to Malta is about three hundred miles of straight flight, so the aircraft had plenty of fuel margin to permit a detour round Sicily instead of going over the top. Why did Pat accept the risk of altimeter failure in fog? And why was he between five and ten degrees off course to port, a line which took him close to Messina instead of over the middle of the island, with Malta right ahead? Like others of our ilk he had acquired a reputation for boldness, particularly as a horseman. In Wexford, an obstacle which no sensible person would attempt was called a Pat Fence; but in an aeroplane, as in one of Beatty's ships, the skipper cannot afford bravura. Could the death throes of Borodale have affected him enough to disturb his judgement?

I have suggested that, at least since Mary Longfield, and probably long before her time, people sometimes behaved oddly, to put it mildly, under the mysterious yet powerful influence which I myself often felt yet never rationalised. Then would it not be likely that the beam, or whatever it was, worked on the succession of owners, so that Pat, being the last of us, was also its last victim? The full-face picture of him which accompanies the account of his crash shows his Service cap askew, so he probably inherited the same dent in the back of the head for which our Admiral was noted, and which might, conceivably, have something to do with the fey streak they shared.

The question remains open, but I have long been convinced, from personal experience, that there was something outstandingly odd about Borodale in certain conditions of mood, or weather or both. Also I find it impossible not to allow that it affected several other lives, some of them disastrously. If that be the case, then it is as well no trace of human habitation remains in the vicinity; and in my opinion it were standing into danger ever to build upon the site again. There are many tales about it which have no place here, but maybe this one is not irrelevant. About the time that Pat was taking over Borodale, in the legal sense that is, a timber merchant obtained permission to fell some Scotch pines. Local people held this to be impious, a desecration, and that no good would come of it. The merchant went one day to see how the felling was going on, and, as he stood there, a tree fell across him and he died.

So perhaps after all I was fortunate not to succeed, either in living there to carry on the line, or to sell so that some other family would come under the bane. Whatever truth, if any, there may be in it, the cold facts are full of implications, not least in relation to our Admiral. From an international standing as high as Nelson's column, and maybe higher – for Horatio was never a full Admiral, a Statesman or an Earl – Uncle David found himself, within a few years, a very lonely person in private life; and in public a voice crying in the wilderness; represented by the House of Lords. Successive National Governments had no inclination to listen to an old sea-dog obsessed by the absurd notion that, as in the past, without naval supremacy – far beyond anything allowed by the various treaties – the Empire would fall apart in the conflict he knew was coming.

The one bright spot in his life at this time was Young David, who was well set on the ladder and had equalled his father's distinction in being posted, as a junior officer, to the Royal Yacht. Peter also helped as much as he could, and particularly through his bloodstock and racing interests; but the affliction (his own word) was gradually getting worse and would have caused his father some swart remembrances.

The winter at 17 Grosvenor Square must have been bleak indeed – 1935; for David's younger brother, Vandy, was taken ill and died there, leaving the lonely Admiral as the last of what the family called 'the litter', meaning his three brothers and one sister. Of these Charlie had departed first, in 1917. George died on active service in India, and Kathleen, 'Trot', in Winchester General Hospital. It is depressing to survive one's siblings, and more so to be the last of a long line. Morale has to be maintained despite an increasingly cold draught blowing from the tomb, but the Admiral was the last man to be daunted by it. He accepted that he was at last running out of steam, and did not need to dramatise, as Vandy had done in expressing a desire to have two hunt servants at his funeral in Newmarket, dressed in their pink coats, to blow 'Gone Away!' at the committal; as though he were himself a fox. The parson could not have been a hunting man, for he declined to make the necessary arrangements, which struck him as impious, if not pagan.

So much for the fading away of our family in the Admiral's generation, though they were only a small segment of the great circle of friends and acquaintances which he had always enjoyed, ever since those early days in Malta; except of course for the lonely years of Scapa Flow and the Firth of Forth. With Ethel's death that circle had at once shrunk, and now, with the Navy reduced to little more than a token force, and his own interests declining – since he would hunt no more, the big houses which used to be so full of life must have been dreary.

His old friend and closest comrade, John Jellicoe of Scapa, now also an Earl, died in London at a time when Beatty happened to be in bed with influenza and fever. Accustomed to give rather than take orders, he rejected those of his doctor and insisted on accepting the honour of being a pall-bearer. This meant he had to walk three miles beside the catafalque, and it was nearly too much for him. The weather was bitter and he was in full dress. His will to escort the only other man who had commanded the Grand Fleet was imperative, but his constitution was no longer strong enough to complete the course. By the time the cortége reached the foot of Ludgate Hill he was so clearly near collapse that a reporter from *The Star* newspaper took the bold step of breaking through the silent throng on the pavement and going right up to the gun-carriage. No one tried to stop him. He offered Beatty a brandy flask, which the Admiral took without question; so he must have been feeling at the end of his tether. Thanks to the spirit he was able to carry on, but it is quite likely that, without it, he might have had a fatal heart attack there and then; for, in addition to 'flu and fever he already had a cardiac insufficiency.

This persisted, as it was bound to do at his age, after the infection subsided, but he was still well enough to look after his various interests: the Navy first, as usual; but he was also concerned with charities, and aired his views in the Lords. Among other things he was Chairman of the Playing Fields Association, a patron of King's College Hospital, and also of the Dockland Settlements (a rehousing scheme).

With the New Year, preparations were begun for celebration of the King's Jubilee, twenty-five momentous years. They began with a stable international and social system, held together by related royalties. They saw these Houses fall, and on the ruins rise a New Order which threatened Pax Britannica. Only in the late twenties did it become apparent that Britain was recovering from her war wounds, so people in general looked to the thirties for a return of peace and plenty, which would endure. Only a few, and Beatty was among them, appreciated the menace beyond that fair horizon. He never ceased his advocacy, not only of sea-power in the conventional sense, but air power also. The man responsible for the first air reconnaissance at sea was already thinking less in terms of capital ships than of carriers.

Also in January the King became ill with a heart condition which would prove to be malignant, and his condition rapidly deteriorated. On the 20th January the wireless broadcast, 'The King's life is drawing peacefully towards its close'. Around midnight he died.

Though again forbidden by his doctors, Beatty insisted on taking part in the funeral procession on 28th January and walked those weary miles successfully. But his health was now seriously and permanently undermined. One may admire his sense of compulsive duty, expressed by the sentence, 'He was not only my King, he was my friend.' At the same time one may question whether either Jellicoe or George V would have approved, nor the Navy neither. Had he lived to feel the whirlwind the Nation would have needed his unique qualities in an appropriately high office. As his old friend Sir Roger Keyes wrote, 'His wise counsel would have been of the greatest value to the Government. His death is a national calamity.'

In February he could still get about, but the day after his last outing he had another heart attack; and this time there was no alternative to complete bed-rest. At one o'clock next morning, the 11th of March, the heart of the Lion stopped.

IO

ABANDON SHIP

Ethel's death and my coming-of-age had both occurred in 1931, so it had been no surprise when Uncle David's letters ceased; for he was no longer the Uncle who must be obeyed. Despite old wounds and many accidents, mostly with horses, I still regarded him as indestructible; so it was a severe shock when, on the evening of 11th March, 1936, I saw that the first item on the news bulletin which I read for Radio Luxembourg, was 'Death of Admiral Beatty'. There followed a potted obituary, so warm that it could only mean he was as much honoured on the Continent as in Britain or the United States.

Early next morning I set off by car for Ostend via Brussels, thence Dover to London, with no plan but to put myself at the disposal of Young David, suddenly the Second Earl. I found him at 17 Grosvenor Square but the body had already been removed. He told me that his father wished to be buried beside Ethel at Dingley but the Government insisted upon a State Funeral, on the sixteenth. That would give me time to drive back home, pick up morning dress, and ask Lu whether she wished to attend. Fortunately she availed herself of the convention that a woman is under no obligation in such circumstances, which might indeed have proved too much for her. She was sixty-seven.

Arrived at St Paul's cathedral as instructed, a verger led me to the front row of chairs facing north under the dome. They were nearly all empty, but soon filled up, except those reserved for people walking in the procession, including David and Peter.

A few feet in front of us there was an oblong gap in the marble floor, twenty feet above the crypt. Time passed slowly. Women all in black, men with black arm-bands – whether in uniform or not – were now coming down the long nave, silent as a flow of dark water. As always when a large number of people are waiting for something to happen, the atmosphere was tense and eerie; till softly the organ began a fugue, becoming louder until one could sense the sound waves weaving around the arches, shimmering along the Whispering Gallery. They suppressed all other sound, so that if one's eyes were closed the cathedral might have been empty. It made one think about mortality, sacrifice, the victim-victor.

The organ music faded out as from afar came melody in a different mode, the band of the Royal Marines slow-marching up Ludgate Hill. Through it came the rhythm of boots, an order to halt. Then silence as the huge West doors seemed to open of themselves, flooding the nave with light. It was as though the whole west wall vanished away, an effect impressive beyond description. Those doors are twenty-eight feet high and weigh three tons, but are so delicately balanced that they can be operated by two men each side.

The organ pipes spoke again: that incomparable 'dead march' which is nothing of the sort but rather the triumph of life. The packed congregation rose to their feet as a bier to which the coffin had been transferred was escorted eastward, where grave clergy with the Archbishop of Canterbury came to meet it from their stalls. It was draped with the Union Flag which had been flown at *Queen Elizabeth*'s mainmast in 1919: Admiral of the Fleet at the pinnacle of fame. His full-dress hat and sword lay upon it, and at the head stood Officers bearing Orders and Decorations on velvet cushions.

The great doors slowly closed. Bearers lowered the coffin on to broad white canvas bands laid on the floor, then lifted it easily in the slings which naturally formed when the ends of the bands were taken up. Stepping each side of the opening to the crypt, the bluejackets prepared to lower away; but as the coffin began to sink out of sight, the forward band slipped. As the coffin dipped, the man nearest to me nearly lost control. Momentarily, it seemed that the coffin must slide out of the bands and go crashing down, taking him with it. I could have grabbed him, but to move at all was beyond my will power. Somehow he regained control, and, with proper dignity, the Admiral's last vessel sank on an even keel into the depths. The choir was singing:—

He who would valiant be
'gainst all disaster
let him in constancy
follow the Master.
There's no discouragement
shall make him once relent
his first avowed intent
to be a pilgrim.

Tension eased with the coffin out of sight and I became caught up in a flight of ideas, almost a daydream, through which the stately ritual hardly penetrated; until the Archbishop, Cosmo Lang, quoted Stevenson's *Requiem*:—

Under the wide and starry sky
Dig the grave and let me lie:
Glad did I live and gladly die,
And lay me down with a will.

This be the verse that you grave for me,
Here he lies where he longed to be;
Home is the sailor, home from the sea,
And the hunter home from the hill.

Superficially the verses are appropriate, but their deeper meaning seemed a denial of the essence of religion, and would certainly have been rejected by the Admiral. He knew he was going *home*, not underground. As *Punch* phrased it:—

'Pipe, Bo'sun, pipe!
The Admiral is sailing,
Sailing under orders only he can take.'

Particularly for seafaring people, the notion of physical resurrection is absurd. And what happens when an atomic blast leaves nothing at all to resurrect? The Admiral knew about death. He had seen so much of it that he could not fail to recognise continuity of identity through the phases of animation. After Jutland he wept openly when it became necessary to consign a hundred and forty bodies to the sea.[1] His honourable tears would not have been only of sorrow but of pride also; through faith in *le bon Dieu*: not a god of the dead but of the ever-living.

Nelson was not ashamed to weep, and if he had less insight than Celtic blood conveyed to Beatty, he too had no illusions about death being the End. One of his last orders was:—

'Don't throw me overboard, Hardy.'
'Oh, no, certainly not.'
Then, replied his Lordship, 'You know what to do.
And take care of poor Lady Hamilton, Hardy.
Take care of poor Lady Hamilton. Kiss me, Hardy.'[2]

At the very end of the ceremony I had an unforgettable and unique experience when a sudden shaft of sunlight fell on a mosaic inscription under the Whispering Gallery, due north from where I sat. It picked out a single, golden, word: *Vixit*. I knew then, past doubt or argument, that my daydream that the Admiral was 'sailing', not subsiding, was not surmise but observation. The same thing had happened when my father was buried. Because everyone else had gone to the funeral I had been left in the care of Agnes, the cook; but she was busy with the preparation of the conventional 'baked meats'. So I went to play with a pile of sand in which I used to make tunnels. Father appeared, apparently so much himself that I did not think there was anything unusual about his being with me at such a time. He did not speak, but communicated relief, love, and joy; as one who has experienced the release of not having to return to the body any more.

Now I knew that the same thing was coming from the Admiral, so, some months after the funeral I wrote a short poem to remind me of that essence, that spirit, which both had distilled from their heroic lives.

> Not in the pride of greatness bravely borne
> nor in the throbbing of the funeral march,

[1] Private communication from Alfred Philp, Commander's messenger in H.M.S. *Lion* at Jutland.
[2] Oman op. cit., p. 557.

or yet its echoes from the ordered throng,
the solemn, measured tramp, the opened doors.

Not by the pathos of cocked hat and sword,
nor in the challenge of the pilgrims' hymn,
or yet a woman weeping near the vault
which gaped before us under that vast dome.

But *vixit* shone: the rest was shadow-dulled,
noble or common, royalty and friends,
all petrified as history, all transient;
but through and through, transcendent,
gleamed the gold, and in one word
was this man's end denied.

Vixit of course means *lived*, but in this context there is more to it than a dictionary definition or the past tense; for in the life of the spirit there is no past save in so far as one may become identified with it. For in truth all one can ever know are the three nodes of being: here, now and 'I'. Though everchanging they are always with us, *ad infinitum*. In the Admiral's own words, 'Death is but a bend in the road of Life.'[1]

Enquiries at the Office of Works for the Cathedral established that, had the coffin slipped, there would not in fact have been a disaster – thanks to the Duke of Wellington. For when the Iron Duke was similarly honoured the same thing happened and the coffin did crash. After which the Dean and Chapter installed a platform which worked like a lift, so that a coffin could be received only three feet from the floor of the nave and gently wound down after the service. It will not be needed again, for since Beatty joined Jellicoe and Nelson, lack of space has prevented any more burials; though several urns of ashes have been incorporated in the walls, a fact which gives to that farewell ceremony an added poignancy.

In order to confirm my observation of the *vixit* inscription, I later tried to identify it but failed. The Clerk of the Works, in

---

[1] Letter to Ethel 1st March 1917 after a destroyer was mined: 'went out on patrol at 5.30 and at 6.10 she ceased to exist.'

reply to a question as to where it might be found, wrote the following:—

'Your question about how the word *vixit* was suddenly illuminated by a ray of sunlight posed a problem, for none of the Choir mosaic inscriptions contains the word while those under the Dome are in English. However, I think the probable answer is this: before it was destroyed by the North Transept bomb in the last war there was a copy of Wren's well-known inscription over an internal porch there. This, as you will see from the enclosed photostat contained the word *vixit* as part of the phrase *non sibi sed bono publico*.

Yours sincerely,
Robert Crayford
Asst.'

So, for all its apparent objectivity, my vision must have been with the mind's eye and not those in my head. It is not less valid on that account, and the experience itself is the more interesting because of it. Then what does it mean? I knew then, and have never doubted since, that, briefly, I experienced continuity of life, the fact of immortality:—

'Words die as the rich mouth crumbles,
and bronze is bent;
and the singing hulls of ships
are broken at last
by the regular rhyme of the waves;
but the spirit holds fast
above time, through the grave,
the value their being meant.
For love is the vision of value and love penetrates
where the eyes and the hands abdicate;
and the spirit receives the value love weaves within it.
Your only estate is the width of your spirit:
all else is the traffic of thieves.'[1]

[1] W. A. Younger: *The Singing Vision.*

So the legend comes to life, and it no longer matters whether what I saw was an inscription blown to bits in the last war. Both Wren and Beatty laboured not for themselves alone, but for a Service which is senior even to the Royal Navy, and for which the great Cathedral was built.

Hansard 5th May 1936

THE PRIME MINISTER (Mr Baldwin): I beg to move, 'That this House will, tomorrow, resolve itself into a Committee to consider an humble address to His Majesty, praying that His Majesty will give direction that a Monument be erected at the public charge to the memory of the late Admiral of the Fleet, Earl Beatty, as an expression of the admiration of this House for his illustrious naval career and its gratitude for his devoted services to the State.

For the second time within a few months the House is being asked by me to pass a Motion of this description. I know it will gratefully pass this Motion for a permanent memorial to the late Admiral of the Fleet Earl Beatty, as an expression of its sense of gratitude to the second of the two great sailors who bore on their shoulders the immense responsibility of command in the Great War. For nearly half the Great War Lord Beatty served under Jellicoe. From November 1916 until the end of the war he bore upon his shoulders that almost intolerable responsibility, the chief responsibility for the safety of our country. They were both great sailors, different of course, but those differences may well be explored by the historians. For me and for the House today we seek, not to compare or measure, but merely to express our thankfulness that at the time of our country's need two such men as Jellicoe and Beatty were there to respond to the call . . .

When I think of Beatty as the people thought of him, I like to think of another aspect of him familiar to me but much less familiar to his countrymen. Although a public figure, although gifted with all those qualities that attract the admiration of mankind, spectacular qualities we may call them in some ways, yet the man himself was fundamentally a shy man, a man who disliked publicity, who never courted it, and who, I rejoice to think, took no part in any of the controversies which have raged since the war. He kept himself aloof from all those things . . .

Those qualities and a mind attuned to statesmanship were given in full after the war, when he spent more than seven years at the Admiralty at a time of intense difficulty for any Sea Lord, at a time when, in the hands of any lesser man, it might have been impossible to have accomplished what was done; for this great sailor, who had been in command of the greatest naval force the world has ever seen, had in those years immediately succeeding the war to turn the whole of his knowledge and the whole of his skill to reducing that force to the very skeleton of what it had been . . .

MR ATLEE: I rise on behalf of the Opposition to support the Motion which has been so eloquently moved by the Prime Minister . . .

SIR ARCHIBALD SINCLAIR: I rise to support on behalf of my hon. and right hon. Friends the Motion before this House . . . So long as the British Navy sails the seas and so long as its fame endures, the man we called Lord Beatty, the deeds he did and the inspiration he gave will be freshly remembered; and so long will he hold a place of honour in the hearts of the British people.

Question put, and agreed to

Resolved,

"That this House will, tomorrow, resolve itself into a Committee to consider an humble address to His Majesty, praying that His Majesty will give directions that a monument be erected at the public charge to the memory of the late Admiral of the Fleet Earl Beatty, as an expression of the admiration of this House for his illustrious naval career and its gratitude for his devoted services to the State."'

I I

TRAFALGAR SQUARE
21ST OCTOBER 1948

'A little before eleven he (Nelson) went down to his cabin for the last time . . . His desk had been left with his pocket-book lying upon it, and he now added a paragraph to the few professional notes which he had entered earlier, under the date, "Monday, October 21st, 1805." His last writing was a prayer.

"May the Great God, whom I worship, grant to my country, and for the benefit of Europe in general, a great and glorious Victory, and may no misconduct in anyone tarnish it; and may humanity after victory be the predominant feature of the British Fleet. For myself, individually, I commit my life to Him who made me, and may His blessing light upon my endeavours for serving my country faithfully. To Him I resign myself and the just cause which is entrusted to me to defend. Amen, Amen, Amen."[1]

Nearly a century and a half later, at the same hour of the same day, the 'great and glorious victory' was commemorated on a scale not seen since his funeral; with the object of linking the immortal memory with two of his heirs and successors, Jellicoe and Beatty.

Though the entire ceremony lasted but thirty-five minutes its evocative effect was at the time unmistakeable and endures in the national memory.

Four hours after writing his prayer Nelson received a mortal wound and was carried below. Chief Surgeon William Beatty, later Sir William, a native of St Andrews and not related to our

[1] Oman (C): Op. cit.

Admiral, though the coincidence of name is striking, examined Nelson's wound in the back and would not attempt to extract a musket ball which had lodged in the spine, for fear of precipitating the end; already near. He died at about half past four in the afternoon.

When Admiral Beatty confided, 'The greatest mistake a man can make is not to die in the hour of victory,' he must have had Nelson in mind, as well as cynically reflecting upon the comparison of heroic death with the disillusion and heartbreak which prolonged his own life. From this Trafalgar Day, however, the shadows fled away.

'JELLICOE AND BEATTY Memorial in Trafalgar Square. Unveiling by H.R.H. the Duke of Gloucester and dedication by the Archbishop of Canterbury 11 a.m. Trafalgar Day, 21st October 1948.

Memorandum J and B No 1   15th September 1948

1. The following arrangements, which have been agreed by all authorities concerned and approved by the Board of Admiralty are promulgated for information and guidance.

CONTROL
2. Control of the ceremony will be exercised, under the direction of the Fourth Sea Lord, by Captain R. K. Dickson, D.S.O., Royal Navy, Chairman of the Jellicoe and Beatty Memorial Committee, Room 106, Citadel. He will establish a control post with a small staff at Entrance No 6 on the east side of the base of the Nelson column.

OUTLINE OF CEREMONY
There follow ten foolscap pages of meticulous detail for one of the most complex parades ever mounted in such a confined space: hardly as much as a square with sides of a hundred yards, because of the area occupied by the column and the fountains.

At paragraph 34 the Memorandum continues with arrangements for one of the earliest outside television broadcasts:—

'The ceremony will be televised "live" in the London area and recorded for television in the U.S. It will be broadcast "live" in the Light Programme and recorded for Overseas Programmes. It will also be covered by the world-wide Newsreel Companies and the World Press.

35.   Television and newsreel cameramen will be accommodated on a stand at the north-west corner of the east fountain. B.B.C. commentator as requisito (sic).

36.   Press Correspondents will be allotted 12 of the 404 reserved seats, and about another 50 will be accommodated (standing) on a platform built about 35 feet from the George IV statue, behind the easternmost of the three new flower beds against the north wall.

37.   Still cameramen and mobile newsreel cameramen will be "royal rota'd" together to a total of four.

38.   The above arrangements will be made through the normal machinery of the Department of the C.N.I.[1] Everything possible will be done to ensure the dignity of the ceremony is not marred from the point of view of those present by the apparatus of publicity. But for one person who sees or hears it in Trafalgar Square, 100,000 will do so through this apparatus. Everyone concerned is therefore requested to help the Press, etc. as much as possible.

39.   The Air Ministry and the Ministry of Civil Aviation have agreed to ban all flying over the Trafalgar Square area during the ceremony.'

As detachments from the three Services, and their Auxiliaries, came from all over the country there could be no rehearsal. That there was not the smallest hitch in their complicated movements is as much a tribute to them as to the organisers.

Representatives, delegates, and close relatives were set down at No 6 entrance, where a yard-arm had been rigged, by Sea Cadets, to carry a hoist of the famous signal which *Victory* flew as the fleet went into battle: 'England expects every man will do his duty.' Originally it was 'confides', but Mr Pasco, Signal Lieutenant, dared to point out that the word was not in the signal book but *expects* was, and would save seven flags, one for each letter. Nelson replied, 'That will do. Make it directly.' Apart from

---

[1] Chief of Naval Intelligence.

'Close action' it was the last hoist *Victory* made under his command.

At the foot of the column were the wreaths which the Navy League annually provides. The distinguished guests passed them on their left and then walked between a naval Guard of Honour and a line of bluejackets. As each guest reached the Guard Commander in the middle of the line, he ordered the 'Present', and, as the thump of a hundred boots sounded like just two, on the feet of some colossus, saluted with the sword.

The seats for the 404 privileged guests faced west, towards a covered platform which accommodated the ecclesiastical procession from St Martin's-in-the-Fields, headed by the Archbishop of Canterbury and the Bishop of London beside the Chaplain to the Fleet. The choirs of Westminster Abbey and St Paul's Cathedral, in the red robes of their 'royal peculiars'[1] followed, as the bells of St Martin's ran a peal of rejoicing. Then the bands struck up. According to *The Times* of 22nd October 1948; 'The arrival of the contingents making up the parade sounded bravely in the quiet of the square. The massed bands of the Royal Marines made a stirring musical entrance as they took their places above the balustrade to the north. On one side of them were assembled eight trumpeters of the Household Cavalry in their State uniforms, and on the other side were the buglers of the Royal Marines. On the eastern corner by the steps was a detachment of the R.A.F., and on the Western corner one of the Foot Guards in full dress. Finally there arrived the Royal Naval Guard of Honour and the King's Colour party to take up their place in front of the memorial.'

The religious service, timed for only nine and a half minutes, began with the hymn 'Praise my soul the King of Heaven'. Then came this prayer:—

'Almighty God, who in time of our need hast ever raised up men to be our defence upon the sea, we praise thy Holy Name for all those who faithfully served their King and Country in the Royal Navy, especially for thy servants John Rushworth Jellicoe and David Beatty; and may this memorial of their faithful service

[1] Certain churches enjoy royal patronage, among them Westminster Abbey and St Paul's Cathedral. Their choristers are endowed with scarlet, instead of black, under the white surplice.

ever remind us of our humble duty, that, following their good example, we may by Thy Grace so pass through the storms of this troublous world that finally, with them, we may come to the land of everlasting life, through Jesus Christ our Lord. Amen.'

The dedication and unveiling followed, the Union Flags falling from the bronzes simultaneously. The Archbishop then recited Nelson's prayer, and, as he came to the last of the three Amens, the choirs sang:

> 'Eternal Father, strong to save,
> Whose arm hath bound the restless wave.
> Who biddst the mighty ocean deep
> Its own appointed limits keep.
> O, hear us when we cry to thee
> For those in peril on the sea.'

As the flags fell away from the memorial, the fountains, until then inert, shot great jets into the air, which, rising some thirty feet and caught by a gust of wind were converted into spray which would have drenched the choristers had they not been protected by an awning. The sound of the water plunging into the basins was like a breaking wave, and, to make the symbol even more convincing, at that time the clouds came down and a gentle drizzle began to fall.

By contrived coincidence, far away in the West Indies, there was also a Naval Occasion. 'Where Nelson anchored his fleet when pursuing Villeneuve before the famous battle, the Home Fleet today observed the 143rd anniversary of Trafalgar. Admiral Sir Roderick Grigon, C-in-C signalled to the assembled ships, "We live in troubled times, and, as in Nelson's day, it is the duty of the fleet lying at Tobago to be fit and ready to meet the enemy if Fate decrees."

"In June 1805, 27 ships of the line were anchored in Courland Bay. Today the reborn Home Fleet, paying its first visit to the spot, consists of the flagship *Duke of York*, 3 cruisers, 8 destroyers and auxiliary ships." '[1]

---

[1] *Daily Telegraph* and *Morning Post* 22nd October 1948.

Nothing could have pleased Admiral Beatty more than that phrase, 'the *reborn* Home Fleet.'

Royalty withdrew, followed at decent intervals by successive rows of the 'red pass' people whose cars were waiting for them. Finally, the parade marched off by detachments to dismiss in St James's Park.

No one who attended on that day is ever likely to forget the majestic feelings the ceremony aroused. To the country as a whole it came to mean a renaissance of patriotism in the highest sense. People did not pay their respects only to the memory of two Admirals, however distinguished. They participated in an effective communion: future, present and past, of all that is most admirable in human nature; and it is significant in that context that, fifty years after Jutland, in 1966, a third bronze bust was added to the north wall. It represents Viscount Cunningham of Hyndhope, Admiral of the Fleet and First Sea Lord, who, off Malta on 10th September 1943, received the surrender of the Italian navy in circumstances so similar to those in the North Sea in November 1918, that only the smaller scale makes the latter different.

Appropriately, it was the veteran battleship *Warspite* which led in three Italian battleships, *Roma, Italia,* and *Vittorio Veneto*, all from Spezia, to be joined that evening by numerous cruisers and destroyers. *Warspite* had been the newest battleship at Dogger Bank, and at Jutland she was nearly lost when damaged steering gear sent her wheeling into the jaws of the High Seas Fleet at Windy Corner. She was saved by surpassing skill. As Cunningham's flagship she had initiated the Italians, as Jellicoe, and Beatty after him, had introduced the Germans to the reality of sea-power: with the same result, bloodless victory.

A contemporary cartoon shows that the public appreciated the parallel, for Cunningham presents to Britannia a ship in a bottle bearing the legend 'Italian Fleet'. He tells her, with becoming modesty, 'I made this for you, M'am, in the Mediterranean.'

Though apparently in the best of health, Cunningham died suddenly; in a taxi on his way to Waterloo to catch a train: 12th June 1963. No doubt he would have been invited to join his peers in St Paul's but for the fact that there was no more room for an interment in the crypt. He was buried at sea, off Portsmouth.

To this day and beyond it, the triumvirate in Trafalgar Square, looking up to their apotheosis at the top of the column he ascended in 1840, thirty-five years after victory and death, remains as witness to future generations concerning the spirit by which they were inspired. It is more than discipline and beyond duty. When confronted with 'the last enemy' it approaches the sublime. Such is the essence of the Service, and of all heroic tradition rooted in self-sacrifice. As such, Spirit is both the cause and the consequence of civilisation.

'Drake he's in his hammock till the great Armadas come,
(Capten art tha sleepin' there below?)
Slung atween the round shot, listenin' for the drum,
An' dreamin' arl the time of Plymouth Hoe.
Call him on the deep sea, call him up the Sound,
Call him when ye sail to meet the foe;
Where the old trade's plyin' an' the old flag flyin'
They shall find him ware and wakin', as they found him long ago!'

Sir Henry Newbolt

THE SERVICE RECORD

Abstracted from vol ii The V.C. and D.S.O. pp 60–62 published by Standard Art Book Company, Paternoster Row, E.C.4 c. 1920

'BEATTY, David.

Entered Royal Navy in 1884, was employed on the Nile, in the Sudan, in co-operation with the Egyptian Army under the Sirdar, Sir H. Kitchener, K.C.B. and rendered excellent service in getting the gunboats over the cataract. He was second in command of the flotilla at the forcing of the Dervishes' batteries at Hafir, and exposed to a heavy fire. He took command of the flotilla on Commander Colville being wounded and fought the gunboats in front of the enemy's batteries most persistently and successfully, eventually bombarding their position at Dongola and dismounting their guns. For this service he was mentioned in Despatches and created a Companion of the Distinguished Service Order.

He was mentioned in Despatches by the Sirdar for services with the gunboats employed on the Nile during the operations of 1893 in the Sudan, including the battles of Atbara and Khartum (medal), promoted to Commander and awarded the 4th class of the Order of Medjidie (1898).

As Commander of the Barfleur he showed exceptional tenacity in endeavouring, with 200 bluejackets, to capture the Chinese guns that caused considerable trouble to the forces and inhabitants of Tien-tsin, June 1900. He managed to get close to the guns but a heavy fire therefrom necessitated withdrawing his force. Although twice wounded he still led his men in the attack. He was promoted to Captain in November 1900 for these services. On 28th April 1905 he was created an M.V.O. (Member of the Victorian Order), and on 5th November 1908 was appointed *Aide de Camp* to the King. He became Rear-Admiral on 1st January

1910, was created companion of the Order of the Bath on the coronation of King George V, 19th June 1911.

From 8th January 1912 to February 1913 he was Naval Secretary to the First Lord of the Admiralty. During the Naval Manoeuvres in July 1912 he was Rear-Admiral commanding the Sixth Cruiser Squadron, with his flag in H.M.S. *Aboukir*. He was Rear-Admiral commanding the 1st Cruiser Squadron from 1st March 1913, and on 22nd June was created Knight Commander of the Bath. On 3rd August 1914 he was promoted Acting Vice-Admiral.

Vice-Admiral Sir David Beatty in H.M.S. *Lion* commanded the force engaged with the German squadron in Heligoland Bight on 28th August 1914, which resulted in the destruction of the German cruisers *Mainz, Ariadne* and *Köln*, and several destroyers.

For his services in the battle of Jutland, 31st May 1916, Admiral Beatty was created a Knight Commander of the Victorian Order and was mentioned by Sir John Jellicoe in his Despatch dated 6th July 1916.

Sir David Beatty was created a G.C.B. in 1916 and a G.C.V.O. in 1917. He commanded the Grand Fleet from 1916. He was created an Earl in 1919. Earl Beatty is a Grand Officer of the Legion of Honour, and he holds the Order of St George of Russia (4th Class).'

Extract from The Times *of Friday 7th July 1916 by its Naval Correspondent*

'. . . If the cloud of witnesses are as near to us as St Paul thought, the spirits of Nelson and Drake and Blake and the Hoods must have looked on well pleased with their successors and descendants; at the Admirals that are, and were, and the Admirals yet to be. Nelson, some of whose mantle has surely fallen on Lord Beatty, with his swiftness of decision, his power of calculating chances, and taking risks which were hardly risks at all, he knew the game so well.

And if Drake and Nelson are as near us as Sir Henry Newbolt and Admiral Fisher think, why then, they must have been well pleased with that day's work (Jutland battle). And they must have welcomed on the farther shore those who died so gloriously for the King and country and their fellow-men. Great Britain shall not perish while these her sons remain to her, – while, rent asunder by dissensions, Nationalists, Ulstermen, Scotsmen, Welsh and English make common cause against a common enemy. These great seamen – some of them – have died, but their names shall live for ever – the youngest midshipman who went down in the *Queen Mary*, – the Boy Jack Cornwell, Arbuthnot and Hood. Seamen and Admirals, they gave all they had to give, their lives. Surely the cloud of witnesses rejoiced that day! There are no tears on that farther shore, nor any pain. There was nothing but rejoicing. Greater love hath no man than this; and the souls of the righteous are in the hand of God.

> 'Admirals all, they said their say,
> And its echoes are ringing still.
> Admirals all, they went their way
> To the haven under the hill."'

AWARDS ORDERS
DECORATIONS

1. D.S.O. 1896
2. Dongola Expedition medal with clasp 1898
3. Order of Medjidieh 4th Class 1898
4. M.V.O. 4th Class 1905
5. C.B. 1911
6. K.C.B. 1914
7. K.C.V.O. 1916
8. Order of St George 4th Class 1916
9. G.C.B. 1916 G.C.B., Grand Officer of the Legion of Honour
10. G.C.V.O. 1917
11. Grand Officer of the Order of Savoy 1917
12. Grand Cordon of the Japanese Order of the Rising Sun 1917
13. Grand Cordon of the Order of Leopold 1918
14. Croix de Guerre, bronze palm 1919
15. Grand Cross of the Star of Rumania 1919
16. Grand Cross of the Legion of Honour 1919
17. Order of Merit 1919
18. Greek Order of the Redeemer, Grand Cross 1919
19. D.C.L. (Oxon) and LL.D. (Aberdeen) 1919
20. Earldom 1919
21. American D.S.M. 1919
22. Titles conferred by H.M. George V:—Baron Beatty of the North Sea and of Brooksby in the County of Leicester, Viscount Borodale of Wexford, Earl Beatty 1919
23. Chinese Order of the Excellent Crop first Class 1920

24. Panamanian Medal (gold) La Solidarad 1920
25. Grand Cordon of the Order of the Rising Sun with Paulowina 1921
26. Privy Councillor 1927

APPENDIX 'A'

Bloodstream

The following particulars are taken from Mss signed by the Deputy Master of Arms, Ulster, who states, 'Compiled by me from printed books of reference and Ms notes in the Office of Arms, Dublin Castle, 1919.'

From his flagship *Queen Elizabeth* on 12th November 1918, the day after the Armistice, our Admiral wrote lightheartedly, 'I am of the Irish persuasion with a dash of French'. In fact he was almost entirely Celt as shown by the following prunings from our family tree.

Eleven generations from Edward III, King of England, Catrine Blennerhassett married Richard M'laughlin of Ballydowney and their daughter married Miles Martin, an Officer in King William's army who fought at the Boyne and Limerick.

Nine generations from Miles, Elizabeth Martin married David Beatty III (1787–1855).

Twenty-four generations after Conaire à que O'Mulconry, Elizabeth Conroy married John Longfield, and three generations later Mary Longfield married David Beatty IV, our Admiral's grandfather.

Meanwhile, six generations after Richard Moore of Dublin, Edith Chaine, *née* Sadlier of Tipperary, married David Longfield Beatty and became our Admiral's mother.

The 'dash of French' refers to a Longfield who fought for Louis XIV and was suitably rewarded. Hence the French name of their Irish house in County Cork: Longeuville.

When David Beatty III married Elizabeth Martin, her sister Mary was the wife of Robert Longfield. Their heiress, Mary

Elizabeth Longfield who married David Beatty IV, was therefore his first cousin.

So their eldest son, David V, the first *Longfield* Beatty, our Admiral's father, had a highly charged heredity through several consanguinous families to which his wife added the Sadlier strain.

Because earlier records were lost when the Dublin Four Courts were burned down during the Easter Rising, 1916, there is no extant confirmation that the family used to be minor gentry in Dumfriesshire, Scotland, or that several Beatty brothers joined King William's army, at least one of whom received a grant of land for his services in the campaign which culminated in the Battle of the Boyne, 1690, and the defeat of the Jacobins.

Either he or his son moved to Dublin, no doubt preferring the relative safety of the Pale, for the recorded founder of our tail male had a business in that city. His heirs did not acquire County status until a century after Boyne Water although they were evidently persons of quality in the time of David II, if not before.

As to the origin of the name, the probability is Scots rather than Irish, if only because it occurs in such a variety of spellings: Beatie, Beattie, Batey, Beaty, Batie, etc., whereas the Irish derivation is more restricted, e.g. Betagh (biadhtch), Beatagh. On these and other grounds there seems little substance in Geoffrey Rawson's version:—[1]

'Admiral Beatty sprang from very old Irish stock. There appears to be some doubt as to the origin of the family name. It has been traced to Betagh (etc.) meaning "public victualler", but in the early Anglo-Irish records the Christian names are Norman (!)'

BEATTY: The Tail Male

David Beatty (1)	of Dublin, probably a grandson of one of the Beatty brothers who came from Scotland and fought at the Battle of the Boyne, 1690.
Edward Beatty	of Dublin married, 7 July 1740, Mary Brock of Glasnevin and died 1794.

[1] Rawson (G): *Earl Beatty, Admiral of the Fleet* (Jarrolds c 1933).

David Beatty (2)	of Dublin married, 1782, Olivia Mary Bell, daughter of Sir Frederick Bell.
David Beatty (3)	of Healthfield, County Wexford, 1787–1855, married, 1813 Elizabeth Martin, daughter of John Martin of Kerry.
David Vandeleur Beatty (4)	of Borodale, County Wexford, 1815–1881, 'the Old Master', married, 1838, Mary Elizabeth Longfield of Cork, only child of Robert Longfield of Longueville, Viscount 1800. She died in 1848.

He married 2nd Letitia Alcock (no issue), and 3rd Margaret Charlotte Alcock, daughter of Harry Alcock of Wilton Castle, County Wexford (1851). They had issue Philip Vandeleur, who married Miss Flood and had nine children.

David Longfield Beatty (5)	of Borodale, 1841–1904, 'the Captain' married 1st on 2nd June 1871, Katrine Edith Chaine, divorced wife of Major William Chaine, 4th Hussars, *née* Sadlier of Dunboyne Castle, County Meath and Nelson's Place, Tipperary.

He married 2nd, Anita Elizabeth Studdy, 'Mouse', and they had one son, Henry, 'Pat', who died 1935. By his first marriage there was issue:—

Charles Harold Longfield, 'the Major', 1870–1917, who married, 30th June 1905, Lucy Alice Langlands, 'Lu', widow of Captain John S. Langlands and daughter of Edward Beck, co-founder of Beck's Bank, Shrewsbury and Welshpool, later incorporated by Lloyds. They had one child, Charles

Robert Longfield, born 1910, (the author.)

David Richard (6), 'the Admiral', 1871–1936, who married, 22nd May 1901, Ethel Field Tree, divorced wife of Arthur Magie Tree of Chicago and only daughter of Marshall Field, also of Chicago. They had two sons, David (7) who became the second Earl, and Peter.

Vandeleur, 'Vandy', Major and Newmarket Trainer, who married twice but had no issue.

George, Indian Cavalry, 30th Jacob's Horse, who married and had issue.

Kathleen Roma, 'Trot', who married Miles Courage and had three sons.

The Tail Male, eldest son to eldest son, becomes extinct on the death of Charles Robert Longfield Beatty. The cadet branch continues through the third Earl, David (8) and his heirs. He has two sons, Shane and Peter.

APPENDIX 'B'

BASTARDY: Legal Considerations

From a written legal opinion, too long to quote, the following answers to, or comments on, the key questions emerge in summary form with the author's wording.

Q: Had the secret leaked, how might their birth out of wedlock have affected the lives of Charles and David Beatty?

A.1. Despite their mother's false declaration on the marriage certificate, giving her status as 'spinster' instead of 'divorced', the marriage of the parents was valid for all five children of David Longfield Beatty and Edith Chaine *née* Sadlier, of whom only the two oldest were illegitimate.

Though under canon law a divorcée is barred from marriage in church the ceremony remains valid as a *fait accompli*.

A.2. Had it been known that Charles and David were bastards neither could have inherited the entailed estates; principally Borodale, Co. Wexford, and in the City of Cork. It would not have been necessary for one or more of the legitimate children to prove a claim, since bastards had no right of inheritance at all.

A.3. Bastardy was not a bar to the King's Commission, but, had it been realised in David's case he would hardly have benefited so much from influence in high places.

A.4. Though legal, the grant of an hereditary peerage might not have been proposed by the Government of the day, nor approved by the Monarch. The question of a coat of arms attached to the Earldom is not a legal issue, so is the subject of a separate note (following).

A.5. Had David, knowing it to be untrue, assured his wife that, if his elder brother died without issue, he would inherit the entailed estates; she could not claim that their marriage was invalid on the ground of false pretences; nor, under English law, would such misrepresentation constitute grounds for divorce.[1]

---

[1] *Author's note*: Had Ethel discovered the truth it would, however, have given her more power over him.

APPENDIX 'C'

BASTARDY: Heraldic Considerations

According to the law of Arms, a bastard may display the shield provided an 'achievement' is added to 'difference' it from the legitimate line. This was not done for Charles or David, who were not, therefore armigerous; though their father was.

Indeed, he was entitled to two shields, the older with only a beehive, the newer quartered with Longfield through his father's marriage to their heiress. The crest on both consists of a lion grasping the crescent (moon).

So, until the granting of his earldom in 1919 the Admiral bore no arms, and the coat was then varied by the College of Heralds to display a cross of St George above the beehive. Supporters were added: a Marine and a Sailor. The crest was still the lion, but he now carried in his dexter paw 'a wreath of the colours' (azure and rouge). A certified copy of the Grant of Arms is preserved in the Maritime Museum at Greenwich and bears this crest, but Debrett's Peerage and other reliable sources also give the old crest; the symbolism of which is not without interest: the solar lion and male principle grasps the lunar and female principle, ruler of the waves.

Until the outbreak of the second great war it was usual for Landed Gentry to display heraldic insignia, despite the risk of prosecution if they failed to pay the tax called Armorial Bearings. Nobility differed from gentry in that the latter, though entitled to such indulgences as a flag over the mansion, a crest on the carriage doors, seldom affected more than such modest applications as crested silver, signet rings, writing paper and seals. Only heirs might wear a gold signet. Others in the line of succession wore the crest cut into a garnet.

APPENDIX 'D'

OPTHALMIA NEONATORUM

The following observations are extracts from a book by R. S. Morton, published in the USA by Sunders in 1977 under the one-word title *Gonorrhoea*. His views are shared by British doctors consulted by the author.

Chapter 6: *Gonorrhoea* in Babies Infants and Children

Gonococcal opthalmia is predominantly a preventable medical problem. *G conjunctivitis* in adults is rare and is usually acquired by auto-inoculation. Babies' eyes are infected by the mother whose secretions, including *lochia*, contain *gonococci*. These organisms usually come from infected cervical glands, some of which are opened by surgical dilation and the pressures of the child as it makes its way through the birth canal.

Opthalmia neonatorum is defined in the U.K. as inflammation of the conjunctivae of the newborn within 21 days of birth. The causes are several. Of the bacterial causes, the *Staphylococcus pyogenes*, *Haemophilus influenzae*, and *Moraxella lacunata* feature most prominently. *Chalmydia A* is nowadays said to account for half the cases. The incidence of *gonococcal opthalmia* is one guide to estimating the degree of control of *gonorrhoea* in a country . . .

The incubation period of *gonococcal opthalmia* is usually two to five days but may be longer. In contrast to most other organisms causing *neonatal opthalmia* the *gonococcus* tends to produce acute and *fulminating conjunctivitis*. (*Staphylococcus pyogenes* is the most notable exception and then only very occasionally) . . .

Incidence of Blindness
    The committee on *opthalmia neonatorum* of the National Society

for the prevention of blindness in the U.S.A. (1973), together with other interested bodies, recommends the continued use of one per cent Silver Nitrate prophylactically. For fear of promoting bacterial resistance antibiotics are *not* recommended for this purpose . . .

Conjunctivitis

The conjunctivitis, usually recorded simply as 'sticky eyes', developed within four days of birth in 36 cases (out of 48; in Glasgow 1964/8). There may be no noticeable symptoms in either males or females.

Meningitis

Can be produced by almost any pathogen from influenza to syphilis, including gonorrhoea, and (eventually) produce symptoms.

CONCLUSION

Whatever the specific organism which caused Peter Beatty's eye trouble, from which eventually he did go blind, it was probably caught at birth from his mother. She need not have known, being symptom-free both before and after the birth, but the complication of meningitis does suggest a gonococcal origin, the source of which could hardly have been the Admiral.

C.B.

APPENDIX 'E'

BORODALE

Originally called Roxanna, the house was built of local stone in the mid-eighteenth century and later the walls were covered with roughcast. The river, about two hundred yards to the south, runs turbulently through a rocky gorge, past a Neolithic fort on a small natural hill ringed with four concentric ditches, of which the lowest would have been full of water. Later, Danish invaders occupied the defences, and various other groups either so employed its tactical value or, it is said, worked the gold from which it takes its name, Dunamore, the hill of gold.

The Admiral's father extracted a certain amount of gold dust from gravel at that point, but there was no prospect of commercial exploitation, so the samples were mounted on paper and put away.

The whole area, including the house, is reputed to be badly haunted, and the hill itself, said to be hollow (and there is some evidence for this), is regarded as a Dûn of the Ever-living, the People of the Sidhe – not to be confused with the Little People. They protect those who honour them and ruthlessly pursue those who deny them.

The following particulars are taken from a brochure issued by the Estate Agents, Battersby & Co., of Westmoreland Street, Dublin, when, having attained my majority and broken the entail, the estate was put up for sale:—

'A VERY CHOICE PROPERTY CONVENIENTLY SITUATED IN THE SOUTH OF IRELAND

Enniscorthy   County Wexford

This very attractive and important Country Seat enjoys a very fine position in the centre of a good agricultural district, well above sea level, surrounded by and overlooking the Estate which comprises 321 acres, all in hand. The Residence is approached by a pleasant winding Avenue with pretty views of the River Boro, which runs through the Demesne, and there are two Entrance Lodges.

The booklet goes on to list the accommodation, including twelve bedrooms, stabling for twenty-four horses, including the Stud Farm, and various outbuildings. There were five cottages in addition to the two Lodges.

When destruction of the house and outbuildings was complete and the weeds had moved in, there was hardly a trace of where the walls had stood.

APPENDIX 'F'

NAMES OF H.M. SHIPS

Throughout the history of the Royal Navy the names of ships frequently recur, particularly in reference to reigning monarchs and their kin. The study of such names is a speciality in itself, and outside the scope of such a work as this; but it is germane in relation to ships associated with our Admiral. Thus, his first ship, *Britannia* represents, for obvious reasons, a number of vessels; and his last, *Queen Elizabeth* is typical of those named after Elizabeth I. *Alexandra* refers to Edward VII's Queen. *Lion* and *Tiger* derive from the animals, as Admiral Fisher confirms:—

> 'There's a terrible outpourin'
> when the Lion is a roarin'
> and the Tiger is a lashin'
> of her tail.'

The abstract idea of character accounts for such names as Indomitable, Inflexible and so forth; though Inconstant seems an odd choice in that context. Destroyers follow a different rule because they are names by classes, each beginning with a different letter, from *Ajax*, *Ardent* and so on to *Venetia*, *Wren* and their ilk.

It was quite usual for a ship having a special role to be replaced by another with a different name which is then rechristened. In this way their identity continues as though the original enjoyed a kind of immortality. *Britannia*, for instance, was accepted as the original First-rate of Trafalgar, but:—

'The *Britannia* was established as a training ship at Dartmouth in 1863, and was joined by *Hindoustan* a year later. In 1869 the original *Britannia* was superseded by a bigger ship, *Prince of Wales*, which, to maintain the tradition, was rechristened *Britannia*. Even after the opening of the College these vessels were retained for technical instruction until, in July 1916, when the demands and losses of war had rendered Britain's supplies of metal dangerously low, they were towed out of harbour to be broken up for the sake of their copper. The whole College mustered on the embankment to witness their passing.'

Wheeler-Bennett (J. W.): *King George V* p47

BIBLIOGRAPHY

So wide is the field of this subject that a bibliography would entail a separate exercise, so the following sources are but random examples to indicate its extent. Periodicals often evoke, better than books, the climate of thought and feeling in times past. In this respect *Punch* and the *Illustrated London News* are particularly effective.

Albion (R. G.): *Forests and Sea Power* Alexander (M): *Phantom Britain* (Muller 1975) Asimov (A): *The Golden Floor* (United States 1865–1918) Bacon (Sir R): *Life of Lord Jellicoe* Baldwin (H): *World War One* (Hutchinson 1963) Balfour (G): *The Battle of Jutland* Bingham (B): *The Falklands, Jutland and the Bight* Bowen (D): *Encyclopaedia of War Machines* (Ed) Octopus 1978 Broad (L): *Winston Churchill, the Years of Preparation* Brookes (E): *Destroyer* (Jarrolds 1962) Bulle (A. H.): *The Navy in Battle* Chalmers (W. S.): *Life and Letters of David Earl Beatty* (Hodder 1951) Chatfield (Lord): *The Navy and Defence 2 vols* (Heinemann) *Keil and Jutland* Churchill (R): *Winston S. Churchill* several vols Churchill (W. S.): *The River War, World Crisis* 2 vols and other works Corbett and Newbold: *Official History of Naval Operations 3 vols* Cross (C): *The Fall of the British Empire* Cunningham (Admiral): *A Sailor's Odyssy* Dewar (K. G. B.): *The Navy from Within* Divine (D): *The Blunted Sword* Duchess of Westminster: *Grace and Favour* Dulles (F. R.): *The United States since 1865* Fawcett and Hooper: *The Fighting at Jutland* Fighting at Jutland (the): *Personal Experiences of Sixty Officers* Filson Young: *With the Battle Cruisers* (1921) Foster (F): *The Perennial Religion* (Regency Press 1969) Franklyn (J): *Shield and Crest* Freemantle (E.R.): *The Battle of Jutland* Frothingham (T. G.): *The Naval History of the World War* (Harvard 1924) 3 vols German Official Account of the Battle of Jutland (Admiralty trans.) Gilbert (M): *Winston S. Churchill 5 vols* Harper (J. E. F.): *Record of the Battle of Jutland* Harvold (C): *Napoleon in Egypt* Hase (von): *Keil and Jutland* Hibbert (C): *Edward VII* (Allen Lane 1956) Hough (R. A.): *Admirals in Collision, First Sea Lord* (Fisher), *The Mountbattens* Irving (J): *The Smoke Screen of Jutland* (Kimber 1966) Jellicoe (Sir John): *The Grand Fleet 1914–1916* (Cassell 1919) Judd (D): *George V* Keyes (Sir Roger): *Naval Memoirs, Adventures Ashore and Afloat* Kilmuir (Lord): *Political Adventures* Leslie (Sir Shane): *The Epic of Jutland* Lewis (M): *Spithead* Lloyd George (D): *The Truth about the Peace Treaties* Longford (E): *The Royal House of Windsor, Victoria R.I.* Macintyre (D): *Jutland* Magus (Sir Philip): *Edward VII* (John Murray 1964) Marder (A. J.): *From Dreadnaught to Scapa Flow* 3 vols O.U.P. 1966 Massie (A. K.): *Nicholas and Alexandra* McElwel (W): *Britain's Wasted Years 1918–1940* Moorehead (A): *The White Nile* Newbolt (H): *Naval Operations 5 vols* O'Brian (M & C): *A Concise History of Ireland* Pastfield (J. L.): *New Light on Jutland* Pitt (B): *The Edge of the Battle* Portland (Duke of): *Memoirs of Racing and Hunting* Plumb (J. H.): *The Court at Windsor* Ramm (A): *Germany 1789–1919* Rawson (G): *Earl Beatty, Admiral of the Fleet* (Jarrolds c 1931) Reuter (Admiral von): *Scapa Flow* Roberts (C): *The Years of Promise* Roskill (S): *Naval Policy between the Wars* 2 vols, *Churchill and the Admirals* (Collins 1977) Sims (W. S.): *Victory at Sea* Smith (P. C.): *Destroyer Leader* Thomson (G. M.): *The Twelve Days* (24 July to 4 August 1914) The V.C. and D.S.O. 3 vols: *Standard Art Book Co* c 1922 Tirpitz (Admiral von): *Memoirs* Tree (R): *When the Moon was High* Waldeyer Hartz (H von): *Admiral Hipper* (trans Holt. Rich & Cowan 1933) Wadham Smith: *The Great Hunger* Warner (P): *Dervish* (MacDonald) 1978 Warner (W): *Cunningham of Hyndhope* (John Murray 1967) Westerman (P. F.): *With Beatty off Jutland* Wheeler-Bennett: *King George VI* (MacMillan 1958) Wingate (F. R.): *Mahdism and the Egyptian Sudan* Woodward (E): *Great Britain and the German Navy* Younger (W): *The Singing Vision* (Hutchinson 1960) See also bibliographies in principal source books, notably Rear-Admiral W. S. Chalmers: *Life and Letters of David Earl Beatty*

INDEX